STRATEGIC PRAYER

BIBLICAL PRAYER

STRATEGIC

EFFECTIVE PRAYER

PRAYER

PROPHETIC PRAYER

CALEB AGADAGBA

A BOLD TRUTH Publication
Christian Literature & Artwork

Strategic Prayer

Copyright © 2018 Caleb Agadagba
ISBN 13: 978-0-9998051-5-2

■ First Edition ■

BOLD TRUTH PUBLISHING
(Christian Literature & Artwork)
606 West 41st, Ste. 4
Sand Springs, Oklahoma 74063
www.BoldTruthPublishing.com

Available from Amazon.com and other retail outlets.
Orders by U.S. trade bookstores and wholesalers.
Email: *boldtruthbooks@yahoo.com*

Quantity sales special discounts are available on quantity purchases by corporations, associations, and others. For details, contact the publisher at the address above.

Cover art by Esthetic Communications.
Formatting and design by Aaron Jones.

Printed in the USA.
03 18   10 9 8 7 6 5 4 3 2 1

Permissions

Dedication

Our Lord & Savior Jesus Christ

To our Lord and Savior Jesus Christ, the originator and source of all things, the greatest person to ever walked the face of the earth, the One Whose teachings on prayer and practical prayer life as recorded in the Bible is unparalleled, without Him this book would not have been conceived! Thank You Lord for paying the price.

My Wife

To my wife, my beloved wife, Pastor Tina Agadagba, a co-laborer in the vineyard of God, a General in God's Praying Army, an intercessor in the body of Christ, a woman of love, faith and a defender of the faith. Thank God for His grace in your life and thank you for your unflinching support and encouragement in getting this vital book out! The Lord multiply His grace in your life in Jesus' Name.

My Daughters

To my daughters; Juliet and Isabel Agadagba, my jewels! A very big thank you for the support both of you have given to me for the work of the ministry. The Lord bless and reward both of you greatly in Jesus' Name.

Acknowledgements

Our accomplishment in life can always be linked to what others have contributed in our lives over the years. I will like to thank the following people that I have been privileged to have in my life.

- My loving wife Pastor Tina and daughters Juliet and Isabel for their unflagging support over the years in the kingdom business of our Lord and savior Jesus Christ. This book would not have been possible without their support.

- My beloved spiritual Father and General Overseer of The Redeemed Christian Church of God, Pastor Enoch Adeboye. A distinguished General in God's Praying Army, a General of Generals in God's vineyard. Thank you, daddy, for all your undiluted teachings especially in the subject of prayer and your practical prayer and fasting life. The Lord continues to strengthen you in Jesus' Name.

- My senior pastors and spiritual mentors; Dr. James Fadel and Pastor Kamal Sanusi. The support, love, and instructions, I have received from both of you over the years has contributed immensely to my development. Thank you, sirs!

- Love Church and Chapel of Restoration leaders, workers and church members. Thank you for allowing me to be your pastor through your submission to the ministry. The Lord reward your labor of love in Jesus' Name.

Contents

Contents

Preface

[Before you read]

This book is intended for believing Christians whose foundation is solely in the Lord Jesus, that is; those who have made Jesus Lord of their life and are faithfully serving Him in truth and in spirit. If you have not yet make Jesus the Lord of your life, please take a moment and do so right now because the next second, minute, hour, day, month or year may just be too late for either of the following reasons:

• No one knows when he or she will depart this world to eternity. Death is inevitable and can come at any time, and after death comes God's judgment as written in the Bible *Book of Hebrews 9:27.*

• No one knows when Jesus will come back to take His saints [believing Christians] home to Heaven. Jesus said even the angels do not know the day or hour of His second coming. (See Bible *Book of Matthew 24:36.)*

Everything does not end here on Earth (this world), that is why the Bible says in *1 Corinthians 15:19 [NKJV] "If in this life only we have hope in Christ, we are of all men the most pitiable."* There is life after death. Eternity is real and can only be spent in one of two places: Hell or Heaven. I want you to take the following question as a food for thought; *"If I die now, where will I spend eternity?"* God's desire is for us to spend eternity in Heaven. Jesus is the only way to spending eternity in Heaven with God, *Acts 4:12.* That is why God sent Jesus [His Son] to die for our sins, so we can have everlasting life—if we believe and make Jesus Lord of our life, *John 3:16, 18.*

> *Acts 4:12 [NKJV]*
> *Nor is there salvation in any other, for there is no other name under heaven given among men by which we must be saved.*

> *John 3:16, 18 [NKJV]*
> *16 For God so loved the world that He gave His only begotten Son, that whoever believes in Him should not perish but have everlasting life.*
> *18 He who believes in Him is not condemned; but he who does not believe is condemned already, because he has not believed in the name of the only begotten Son of God.*

~

"If I die now, where will I spend eternity?"

The Word of God [the Bible] tells us that if you confess with your mouth the Lord Jesus and believe in your heart that God has raised Him from the dead, you will be saved [that is; you become born again]. See Bible reference below.

> *Romans 10:9-10 [NKJV]*
> *9 That if you confess with your mouth the Lord Jesus and believe in your heart that God has raised Him from the dead, you will be saved.*
> *10 For with the heart one believes unto righteous-*

ness, and with the mouth confession is made unto salvation.

To be born again, please say the prayer below:

Prayer of Salvation

"Lord Jesus, I believe in my heart that You died and was buried and God raised You from the dead for my salvation. I repent from my sins and receive forgiveness, and I confess with my mouth Your Lordship over my life. Thank You, Father God, for sending Your Son Jesus for my salvation, in Jesus' Name I pray, Amen."

Praise God, you have just been transformed from death to life everlasting. You've been justified by God's grace through your faith in Jesus. You are now in right standing with God. Welcome to the precious family of God's children. You are now an heir of God the Father and a joint heir with the Son, Jesus Christ. See bold text in Scripture below. *Romans 8:17, Titus 3:7.*

Romans 8:17 [NKJV]
*And if children, **then heirs; heirs of God and joint heirs with Christ,** if indeed we suffer with Him, that we may also be glorified together.*

Titus 3:7 [NKJV]
*That having been justified by His grace **we should become heirs** according to the hope of eternal life.*

Strategic prayer points and Declarations

STRATEGIC PRAYER

■ 1. Pray for the salvation of the following people listed below, because there is no profit when we get everything the world can offer, become wealthy and famous, but at the end of time lose the most vital part of us; our soul. *Matthew 16:26 [NKJV] "For what profit is it to a man if he gains the whole world, and loses his own soul? Or what will a man give in exchange for his soul?*

• Salvation of your family members; spouse, children, siblings, parents, etc.

• Salvation of your friends: work friends, school friends, friends in your neighborhood, etc.

• Salvation of those who are yet to accept Jesus as Lord and Savior around the world.

■ 2. Pray the following points listed below in the life of your loved ones so that when the Gospel is preached to them it will not be hindered. *2 Corinthians 4:4 [NKJV] "Whose minds the god of this age has blinded, who do not believe, lest the light of the gospel of the glory of Christ, who is the image of God, should shine on them."*

• Spiritual deafness restored, so that they will hear and understand.

• Spiritual blindness restored, so that they will see and perceive.

• Their heart is prepared and ready to receive the Word of God.

■ 3. Pray that your mouth will always be filled with praise and thanksgiving to God, *Psalms 34:1 [NKJV] "I will bless the Lord at all times; His praise shall continually be in my mouth.."*

■ 4. Pray that the Word of God makes rapid and tremendous advancement in the world, especially in places where the gospel of Jesus Christ is being hindered. *Acts 19:20 [NKJV] "So the word of the Lord grew mightily and prevailed."*

■ 5. Pray for God's Kingdom to come and His will be done in your life, family, loved ones, and your nation and on earth. *Matthew 6:9-10 [NKJV] "9 Our Father in heaven, hallowed be your name. 10 Your kingdom come. Your will be done on earth as it is in heaven."*

STRATEGIC DECLARATIONS

■ 1. According to *John 1:12*, I am a child of God because I was given the right to become a child of God when I accepted Jesus as Lord and Savior. God is my Father and nobody or devils in darkness can revoke it in Jesus' Name. *John 1:12 [NKJV] "but as many as received Him, to them He gave the right to become children of God, to those who believe in His name."*

■ 2. According to *John 1:13*, I am not born of blood, nor

of flesh, nor of the will of a man, but of God; therefore I am no more under the subjection of earthly genetic related blood diseases or earthly ancestral curses and manipulations, rather I operate under the principles of God's Kingdom which are: righteousness, peace and joy in the Holy Spirit as written in *Romans 14:17 (NKJV) "for the kingdom of God is not eating and drinking, but righteousness and peace and joy in the Holy Spirit." John 1:13 [NKJV] "who were born, not of blood, nor of the will of the flesh, nor of the will of man, but of God."*

■ 3. By the grace of God, I am a citizen of Heaven, therefore I am not under the control of the world system and its influence. I declare an open Heaven continually over my life and loved ones. *Philippians 3:20 [NKJV] "For our citizenship is in heaven, from which we also eagerly wait for the Savior, the Lord Jesus Christ."*

■ 4. I am seated in heavenly places in Christ Jesus. High above all principalities and powers of this world. *Ephesians 2:6 [NKJV] "And raised us up together, and made us sit together in the heavenly places in Christ Jesus."*

■ 5. I refuse to be under the control of drugs, alcohol, pornography, anger, hate, unforgiving spirits, etc. *Romans 6:14 [NKJV] "For sin shall not have dominion over you, for you are not under law but under grace."*

■ 6. I have been made alive by Jesus, I am not dead in sins and trespasses anymore. *Ephesians 2:1 [NKJV] "And you*

He made alive, who were dead in trespasses and sins."

■ 7. I am no longer under the influence of the spirit of disobedience. In Jesus' Name I declare deliverance upon my family members who are still under the control of the spirit of disobedience. *Ephesians 2:2 [NKJV] "in which you once walked according to the course of this world, according to the prince of the power of the air, the spirit who now works in the sons of disobedience."*

■ 8. I am crucified with Christ, It is no longer I who live but Christ lives in me. The life of Jesus will be demonstrated to the world through me. *Galatians 2:20 [NKJV] "I have been crucified with Christ; it is no longer I who live, but Christ lives in me; and the life which I now live in the flesh I live by faith in the Son of God, who loved me and gave Himself for me."*

■ 9. I no longer walk and live according to the course of this world and according to the prince of the power of the air, rather I now walk and live by faith in Jesus Christ, Who loved me and gave Himself for me, praise God.

■ 10. I am born of God and cannot be under the influence of the nature of sin because God's seed (DNA) is in me, praise God. *1 John 3:9 [NKJV] "Whoever has been born of God does not sin, for His seed remains in him; and he cannot sin, because he has been born of God."*

■ 11. Sin cannot have dominion over me because I am

not under the law but under grace in Jesus' Name, Amen. *Romans 6:14 [NKJV] "For sin shall not have dominion over you, for you are not under law but under grace."*

■ 12. I have been washed and saved from my sins by the blood of Jesus. I am righteous and will not succumb to sin and its reproaches in Jesus' Name, Amen. *Matthew 1:21 [NKJV] "And she will bring forth a Son, and you shall call His name Jesus, for He will save His people from their sins."*

■ 13. I have been justified by the blood of Jesus and as such I am saved from wrath. Praise God. *Romans 5:9 [NKJV] "Much more then, having now been justified by His blood, we shall be saved from wrath through Him."*

Introduction

Like a vehicle or bicycle pedal, Prayer can be said to be the spiritual pedal of the believer. The pedal is used for accelerating a vehicle by getting more gasoline to the engine. Many believers are decelerating, and some have come to a stop, and are grounded because they have taken their foot off the spiritual pedal (prayer).

Nowadays prayer has been relegated in the church, family, ministry and in individual Christian lives. Churches don't pray as they used to do, and the topic of prayer is hardly taught in churches and Christian meetings. Even the few that pray, don't pray strategically. We are raising believers who don't know how to talk to the One they believe in! This is in sharp contrast to what Jesus said concerning prayer in *Luke 18:1*, that believers should always pray and not to give up.

Churches are always parked for food and entertainment related meetings but not for prayer and fasting meetings! This is not supposed to be so. Imagine living without a cell phone in this modern age! Frustrating isn't it? Off course very frustrating because you cannot easily get things done. That is what it is like being a Christian without prayer in our life! And this is what most Christians are like these days because they don't communicate in prayer with the God they believe in.

God is not just God only as most people see Him, but He is also the heavenly Father to those who believe in Jesus Christ as Lord and Savior. That is why Jesus said to His disciples in *Luke 11:2*, that when praying they should say *"Our Father who is in heaven."* Just as earthly fathers want their children to communicate with them, so our heavenly Father wants us (believers) to communicate with Him, and prayer is the medium by which believers communicate with their heavenly Father.

As you read his book, your prayer life will be strengthened because you will learn how to pray strategically, improve your communication with God, grow to become a spiritual giant in the body of Christ, and help strengthen other believers by teaching them how to pray strategically.

$\sim$

Chapter 1
What is Strategic Prayer?

Prayer is the art of talking to God in accordance with His Word in order that His will be carried out here on Earth. It is the line of communication between God and human beings. Prayer is a spiritual phenomenon carried out by the physical body. When we pray to God, we communicate with our spirit; our body (mouth) is the medium by which the communication made in our spirit comes out as sound.

The majority of us in the body of Christ [believing Christians] have been suffering numerous defeats at the hands of the enemy because we launch attacks at the camp of the enemy aimlessly. Most of the time in a united group prayer, people pray without listening to the prayer points and often just speak in tongues instead of paying attention to the prayer points first before praying. This is praying aimlessly, or praying out of order. I am not saying speaking in tongues should not be used during prayer sessions. In fact, speaking in tongues should be encouraged during prayer sessions; in other words Christians gifted with speaking in tongues should deploy it during prayer sessions. However, understanding the prayer points before praying—is key to praying strategically.

Apart from suffering defeats, the volume of our prayers is not directly proportionate to the results we see. There is a huge contrast between the volume of prayers believing Christians offer to God daily compared to the effect of the prayers in the people, society, government, etc. The question is; why is this so? Why the sharp contrast? We must be doing something wrong, because there is nothing wrong with God. We must be praying the wrong way! *James 4:3* says; we pray and do not receive because we pray wrongly for our selfish motives. *James 4:3 (NIV) "When you ask, you do not receive, because you ask with wrong motives, that you may spend what you get on your pleasures."* That is, we are praying without following God's Word on how to pray. God's strategic plans can be found only in God's Word, the Bible. The Bible tells us in *Hosea 4:6;*

> *Hosea 4:6 [NKJV]*
> ***My people are destroyed*** *for lack of knowledge.* ***Because you have rejected knowledge,*** *I also will reject you from being priest for Me; because you have forgotten the law of your God, I also will forget your children.*

The bold sentence above *"my people are destroyed,"* can be translated to mean; *"My people suffer defeat"* while *"because you have rejected knowledge"* can be translated to mean, *"operating without God's strategic plan."* That is; wrong application of God's Word or not applying God's Word at all because of a lack of knowledge of it.

Note, that in *Hosea 4:6*, God said that if we reject His Word, He would reject us from being priests unto Him. Now this is very important because one of the functions of a priest as written in the *Book of Joel 2:17* is to offer intercessory prayers for people and nations.

Joel 2:17 [NKJV]
Let the priests, who minister to the Lord, Weep between the porch and the altar; Let them say, "Spare your people, O Lord, and do not give your heritage to reproach, that the nations should rule over them. Why should they say among the peoples, 'Where is their God?'"

This means that nations and their citizens are exposed to defeat and destruction when the priest appointed over them as intercessors lack the knowledge of how prayers should be deployed. The priests referred to in *Joel 2:17*, are not limited to ordained or commissioned ministers, but rather applies to all believing Christians who have accepted Jesus as Lord and Savior and living daily by Jesus' Word, the Bible. Believing Christians are called priests in the Bible (as seen in *1 Peter 2:9* and *Revelations 5:10*). [See Scripture reference below.] This means as a believer, you are a priest appointed over families, nations, and people of different race, culture, etc., as an intercessor to declare or proclaim the will of God over them.

1 Peter 2:9 [NKJV]
But you are a chosen generation, a royal priesthood, a holy nation, His own special people, that you may

proclaim the praises of Him who called you out of darkness into His marvelous light.

Revelations 5:10 [NKJV]
And have made us kings and priests to our God; and we shall reign on the earth.

Before getting into what strategic prayer is, it is imperative we understand the meaning of the word "strategic." In physical warfare, "strategic" or strategy refers to a detailed plan of action designed to cause maximum destruction in the territory of the enemy with the intention of rendering the enemy incapable of launching a counter attack.

A strategic attack is an attack that is carried out according to a strategic plan. Victory in any battle comes when the battle is launched or fought as per planned strategy. A strategic attack hardly misses its target. It hits right at the desired spot at first launch. Let's look at the 'David versus Goliath' battle in *1 Samuel 17:40, 45,* and *49.*

David had five stones in his shepherd's bag and his sling in his hand when he battled Goliath. He deployed his weapon according to God's Word because, though he had five stones and a sling, his faith was not in the stones and the sling, rather his faith was in God, because when he drew close to Goliath, he engaged God and His Word by saying in *1 Samuel 17:45 NKJV "...You come to me with a sword, with a spear, and with a javelin. But I come to you in the name of the Lord of hosts, the God of the armies of*

Israel..." Because of this, with his slingshot he killed the enemy with one stone; he was right on target—first shot, He did not have to waste time or energy. Strategic prayer is not a short, voluminous or lengthy prayer but rather targeted prayer.

With the above explanations of strategy: strategic prayer can be said to be concerned with praying by God's strategic plan [God's Word] for a specific purpose or purposes, for tremendous impact or results. That is; engaging God's entire armory when praying anytime and every time for any purpose so that God's desired results can be realized. Simply put; strategic prayer is praying the God way. *Ephesians 6:13-18* is a powerful Scripture that buttress the above definition of strategic prayer.

> *Ephesians 6:13-18 [NKJV]*
> *11 Put on the whole armor of God that you may be able to stand against the wiles of the devil.*
> *12 For we do not wrestle against flesh and blood, but against principalities, against powers, against the rulers of the darkness of this age, against spiritual hosts of wickedness in the heavenly places.*
> *13 Therefore take up the whole armor of God that you may be able to withstand in the evil day, and having done all, to stand.*
> *14 Stand therefore, having girded your waist with truth, having put on the breastplate of righteousness,*
> *15 and having shod your feet with the preparation of the gospel of peace;*

16 Above all, taking the shield of faith with which you will be able to quench all the fiery darts of the wicked one.
17 And take the helmet of salvation, and the sword of the Spirit, which is the word of God;
18 Praying always with all prayer and supplication in the Spirit, being watchful to this end with all perseverance and supplication for all the saints.

You can see a clear strategy from the above Scriptures of how prayer should be deployed. Before talking of when and how to pray and the kinds of prayer in *verse eighteen*, it first explains why (specific purpose) we should pray in *verses eleven, twelve,* and *thirteen* and then listed the specific armor that should be in place and what they help us achieve during prayer. This means, *"Prayer is a key weapon used in deploying God's weapons."* Let's take a closer look at the armor listed in *verses fourteen to seventeen.*

~

"Strategic prayer is not a short, voluminous or lengthy prayer but rather targeted prayer."

Waist Girded with Truth

Truth is a vital weapon and amour in strategic praying, because you cannot win any battle if you are in error or operating with the spirit of error [lying spirit]. Truth is having knowledge of the totality of God's Word. Praying in truth keeps you standing: that is, truth gives you the required spiritual energy to stand while praying and helps fuel your faith because the Bible tells us in *Romans 10:17* that faith comes by hearing the Word of God and the Word of God is truth as seen in *John 17:17 "Sanctify them by Your truth, Your word is truth."* The Bible tells us that this powerful weapon of faith suffers serious defeat when we operate in error or lies. See *2 Timothy 2:18* below.

> *2 Timothy 2:18 [NIV]*
> *They have left the true teaching, saying that the rising from the dead has already taken place, and so they are destroying the faith of some people.*

> *2 Timothy 2:18 [NKJV]*
> *Who have strayed concerning the truth, saying that the resurrection is already past; and they overthrow the faith of some.*

∽

"Strategic prayer is praying the God way."

The Bible tells us in *John 8:32* that the truth that we know and operate with is what brings freedom and deliverance. That is; no matter how long we spend in prayer, if we are in error, it will end up fruitless. The Bible also makes it clear to us that no man can do anything against the truth but for the truth, *2 Corinthians 13:8*. This means praying in truth will always lead to victory.

John 8:32 [NKJV]
And you shall know the truth, and the truth shall make you free.

2 Corinthians 13:8 [NKJV]
For we can do nothing against the truth, but for the truth.

~

"Prayer is a key weapon used in deploying God's weapons."

Breastplate of Righteousness

Strategic praying requires that one be in right standing in and with God. Like the weapon of truth, righteousness gives you the right footing while praying. In *Ephesians 6:14* the Word of God says that we should stand therefore with *our waist girded with truth* and with *the breastplate of righteousness* on. It is the prayer of a righteous man that makes tremendous impact and total destruction in the territory of the enemy as seen in *James 5:16*.

James 5:16 [AMP]
Confess to one another therefore your faults (your slips, your false steps, your offenses, your sins) and

*pray [also] for one another, that you may be healed
and restored [to a spiritual tone of mind and heart].
The earnest (heartfelt, continued) prayer of a righteous man makes tremendous power available [dy-
namic in its working].*

Unrighteousness and unrighteous acts give the devil the
right to resist and oppose you even in the presence of God
as seen in *Zachariah 3:1, 3*. The Bible tells us in *James 4:7*
that we have the authority to resist the devil, and when we
do, the devil checks out [flees from us]. But when we engage in unrighteous acts, this authority reverses order as
seen in *Zachariah 3:1, 3* such that instead of us resisting
the devil, he (the devil) ends up resisting us.

Zachariah 3:1, 3 [NKJV]
*1 Then he showed me Joshua the high priest standing
before the Angel of the LORD, and Satan standing at
his right hand to oppose him.
3 Now Joshua was clothed with filthy garments, and
was standing before the Angel.*

∾

"No matter how long we spend in prayer, if we are in error it will end up fruitless."

Righteousness can be said to be the spiritual bullet proof-
ing of a praying Christian, hence *Ephesians 6:14*, says we

should arm ourselves with the breastplate of righteousness before engaging in prayers.

Right standing [righteousness] in and with God requires that one be born again [accept the finished work of Jesus] and live daily by faith in the Word of God [a disciple]. In the preface of this book titled **"Before you read"** I wrote how a person can become born again. *Romans 10:10* tells us how one can become righteous and *John 8:31* tells us how we can become Jesus' disciples.

> *Romans 10:10 [NKJV]*
> *For with the heart one believes unto righteousness, and with the mouth confession is made unto salvation.*

> *John 8:31 [AMP]*
> *So Jesus said to those Jews who had believed in Him, if you abide in My word [hold fast to My teachings and live in accordance with them], you are truly My disciples.*

~

"Righteousness can be said to be the spiritual bullet proofing of a praying Christian."

Gospel of Peace

The plan of the devil is to cause chaos in individuals, families, churches, nations, businesses, etc. The Bible tells us in *John 10:10* that the primary objective of the devil is to steal, kill, and destroy. A person or family in chaos cannot engage in strategic prayers because of the distraction and confusion created by the chaos. Arming ourselves with the Gospel of Jesus Christ, releases peace in our hearts, families, and environment. This gives us the firm footed stability, promptness, and readiness to pray anytime for any purpose with the desired results.

Shield of Faith

Faith is required to quench all the fiery darts [flaming missiles] of the devil. According to *Ephesians 6:16*, faith should be lifted above all other weapons because without faith it is impossible to engage God. *Hebrews 11:6* tells us that without faith, it is impossible to please God, and anyone who comes to God must believe that He is God and that He rewards those who seek Him diligently. In other words, praying without faith amounts to nothing. "Faith is the spiritual law by which the other armor and weapons operates." The Bible tells us in *Romans 3:27* that faith is a law, *Romans 3:27 [NKJV] "Where is boasting then? It is excluded. By what law? Of works? No, but by the law of faith."*

Helmet of Salvation

The helmet of salvation serves two purposes. Firstly, is a protection and secondly it serves as an identification of one who has overcome the world. The Bible says in *1 John 5:4 "...He that is born of God (saved) overcomes the* world…" Putting on *the helmet of salvation* can be said to mean displaying your new status in Christ. Salvation is the starting point of strategic praying because if one is not saved, he or she cannot launch a successful attack on Satan and his emissaries.

~

"Faith is the spiritual law by which the other armor and weapons operates."

The Sword of the Spirit

The Word of God is *the sword of the spirit* as stated in *Ephesians 6:17*. Praying without clear knowledge of the Word of God is un-strategic because it is like fighting in a battle with a defective weapon, or fighting without a weapon. According to *Hebrews 4:12*, It is the Word that makes our prayers effective in the spiritual, soulish and physical realms.

> *Hebrews 4:12*
> *For the word of God is living and powerful, and sharper than any two-edged sword, piercing even to the division of soul and spirit, and of joints and marrow, and is a discerner of the thoughts and intents of the heart.*

In *Jeremiah 23:29*, the Word of God is likened to fire and hammer. Thus, praying with the Word of God during prayer sessions releases fire over Satan's works and breaks down satanic barriers.

Jeremiah 23:29 [NKJV]
Is not My word like a fire?" says the Lord, and like a
hammer that breaks the rock in pieces?

Strategic Prayer Points and Declarations

STRATEGIC PRAYER

■ 1. Pray that you will be armed always with the complete armor of God so that you can withstand and overcome the stratagems of the devil. *Ephesians 6:11 [NKJV] "put on the whole armor of God that you may be able to stand against the wiles of the devil"*

■ 2. Pray that God will grant you the wisdom and revelation to be able to identify who the real enemy in your life is, so that your prayers will always be on target. *Ephesians 6:12 [NKJV] "For we do not wrestle against flesh and blood, but against principalities, against powers, against the rulers of the darkness of this age, against spiritual hosts of wickedness in the heavenly places"*

■ 3. Pray that God will grant you the grace and wisdom to always deploy the right weapon as written in *Ephesians 6:13-18* against Satan, his demons and agents of darkness.

STRATEGIC DECLARATIONS

■ 1. I see myself the way God sees me. My circumstances cannot dictate for me or define me. I am a mighty man [woman] of valor. *Judges 6:12 [NKJV] "And the Angel of the Lord appeared to him, and said to him, "The Lord is with you, you mighty man of valor!"*

■ 2. The Lord Jesus is with me, He has not forsaken me therefore I will not be afraid of the enemy or whatever has happened or is happening to me in Jesus' Name. *Matthew 28:20 [NKJV] "...lo, I am with you always, even to the end of the age. Amen."*

■ 3. I refuse to be under the oppression of Satan, his emissaries, and his agents. I am a deliverer and will deliver myself and family from the hand of the oppressor in Jesus' Name. *Judges 6:14 [NKJV] "Then the Lord turned to him and said, "Go in this might of yours, and you shall save Israel from the hand of the Midianites. Have I not sent you?"*

~

Chapter 2
Our Prayers before God

The majority of believers don't pray because they are igno-rant of how precious their prayers are before the throne of God. Some has even said that God does not hear or answer prayers anymore and therefore they don't pray for their mir-acle. This is a lie straight out of the pit of Hell because God hears and answers prayers that are offered according to His will. See below Scriptures in *1 John 5:14-15* and *Psalms 65:2*.

> *1 John 5:14-15 [NKJV]*
> *14 Now this is the confidence that we have in Him, that if we ask anything according to His will, He hears us.*
> *15 And if we know that He hears us, whatever we ask, we know that we have the petitions that we have asked of Him.*

> *Psalms 65:2 [NIV]*
> *You who answer prayer, to you all people will come.*

One of the reasons many think God no longer answers prayer is because they see God as a man who changes—

God does not change! God said in His Word in *Malachi 3:6* "...*For I am the Lord I do not change...*" In His teachings, Jesus emphatically said that when we ask, seek, and knock, we will receive whatever we ask from the Father in His Name. He said anyone that asks in prayer will receive his answer, he that seeks in prayer will find what he is seeking for and he that knocks in prayer, the door will be opened for him. See Scripture reference below.

Matthew 6:7-8 [NKJV]
7 Ask, and it will be given to you; seek, and you will find; knock, and it will be opened to you.
8 For everyone who asks receives, and he who seeks finds, and to him who knocks it will be opened.

The prayers of believing Christians are precious in the sight of God. God's ears are always open, and He pays close attention when His children are praying to Him. The Bible tells us in *1 Peter 3:12* that God's ears are open to the prayers of Christians.

1 Peter 3:12 [NKJV]
*For the eyes of the Lord are on the righteous, **and His ears are open to their prayers**; but the face of the Lord is against those who do evil.*

Take note of the underline in bold above; it did not say that our prayer is what opens God's ears, but rather God's ears are open to our prayers. Thus, praying for God's ears to be open to our prayers as believers is not strategic praying because—God's ears are always open. All we need to do is to pray in faith and in the Name of Jesus for the need at hand; no doubt, God will hear because His ears are always open to the believer's prayers.

∽

"Jesus emphatically said that when we ask, seek, and knock, we will receive whatever we ask from the Father in His Name."

Now some will argue against this by referring to Solomon's prayer in *2 Chronicles 6:40* where Solomon prayed for God's eyes to be open and His ears attentive to prayers offered in the temple. The word *attentive* should not be mistaken for open. Attentive simply means to pay close attention to something. Under the new covenant of grace, God's ears are always open to the prayers of born again Christians living holy daily by faith. Even David in the old covenant spoke prophetically (as written in *Psalms 34:15)* that God's ears are always open to the cry [prayer] of His children. See Scripture reference below.

Psalms 34:15 [NKJV]
*The eyes of the Lord are on the righteous, **and His ears are open to their cry.***

Our prayers as incense before God

The Bible tells us in *Revelations 5:8* that the four living creatures and the twenty-four elders surrounding the throne of God have golden bowls in their hands full of incense which are the prayers of the saints. See underline in bold below.

> *Revelations 5:8 [NKJV]*
> *Now when He had taken the scroll, the four living creatures and the twenty-four elders fell down before the Lamb, each having a harp, and golden bowls full of incense,* **which are the prayers of the saints.**

Does this mean that as a Christian, my prayers are incense producing sweet odors before the throne of God? The answer is—yes (as seen in *Revelations 5:8*), our prayers are continually before God in Heaven. Praise God, I am counted worthy by the blood of Jesus for my prayers to be accepted as a sweet-smelling incense before God.

~

"Under the new covenant of grace, God's ears are always open to the prayers of born again Christians living holy daily by faith."

The four living creatures and the twenty-four elders before the throne do not rest worshiping God (*See Revelations 4:8, 10*), which means if I continue praying, my prayers are standing for me before the throne as the elders and the living creatures worship God forever and ever with the bowls in their hand—containing my prayers.

Our prayers as memorial before God

Our prayers are serving as a memorial for us before God in Heaven. This was recorded in *Acts 10:1-4* about a devout man Cornelius, whose prayers stood before God as a memorial for him. See Scripture reference below.

> *Acts 10:1-4 [NKJV]*
> *1 There was a certain man in Caesarea called Cornelius, a centurion of what was called the Italian Regiment,*
> *2 A devout man and one who feared God with all his household, who gave alms generously to the people,* ***and prayed to God always.***
> *3 About the ninth hour of the day he saw clearly in a vision an angel of God coming in and saying to him, "Cornelius!"*
> *4 And when he observed him, he was afraid, and said, "What is it, lord?" So he said to him, "Your prayers and your alms have come up for a memorial before God.*

From the above Bible Scriptures in *verse two*, Cornelius' prayers were always before God because he prayed to God always. For our prayers to come before God as a memorial, we must pray to God always. Praying to God always can be said to mean praying on a regular basis like once, twice, thrice or as much as you can every day. In *verse three* above, the angel visited Cornelius about the ninth hour (3pm), called the hour of prayer *(Acts 3:1)*. This tells us that Cornelius was locked up in prayer at the time of the vision.

Strategic Prayer Points and Declarations

STRATEGIC PRAYER

■ 1. Pray the following points listed below over your life and loved ones. *Numbers 23:19-20 [NIV] 19 God is not human, that he should lie, not a human being, that he should change his mind. Does he speak and then not act? Does he promise and not fulfill? 20 I have received a command to bless; he has blessed, and I cannot change it.*

• Pray that God should act on and fulfil every promise He has said in His Word concerning you and your family in Jesus' Name.

• Pray that nothing including you will be able to change God's will for you and your family in Jesus' Name.

■ 2. Pray that God will grant you and believers worldwide divine strategies to enable the penetration of the Gospel to the unsaved.

■ 3. Pray that the work of God worldwide will not lack the required finance for the propagation of the Gospel of Jesus.

STRATEGIC DECLARATIONS

■ 1. I am unshakable and unmovable because my trust is in the Lord God Almighty. *Psalms 125:1 [NKJV] Those who trust in the Lord are like Mount Zion, which cannot be moved, but abides forever.*

■ 2. I declare that wickedness and wicked acts will not rest on me and my loved ones in Jesus' Name. *Psalms 125:3 [NKJV] For the scepter of wickedness shall not rest on the land allotted to the righteous, lest the righteous reach out their hands to iniquity.*

■ 3. According to *1 Peter 2:9*, I belong to Heaven's royal family, I am peculiar and special, I am not ordinary. Therefore, I am determined to demonstrate the glory of God to the world. *1 Peter 2:9 [NKJV] But you are a chosen generation, a royal priesthood, a holy nation, His own special people, that you may proclaim the praises of Him who called you out of darkness into His marvelous light.*

~

Chapter 3
The Praying Vessel

When we pray to God according to His Word, our prayers are supposed to move the hands of God to act on our behalf and produce the desired results. If God is not hearing our prayers or acting on them, it can either be one or both reasons below:

▶ 1. Problem with the vessel [person] saying the prayer.

▶ 2. Problem with the prayer that is being said.

In this chapter we will be focusing on the praying vessel; that is, the person saying the prayer. The prayer that is being said is covered in the chapters of; know what you are praying for, know why you are praying and know how to pray.

The praying vessel can hinder God from acting if he or she plays the double standard, that is; claims to be a Christian but practices sin; that is, engage in activities contrary to God's Word. The Bible tells us in the *Book of Isaiah 59:1-2* that our sins can prevent God from hearing our prayers and make Him to hide His face from us because His eyes are too holy to behold iniquity.

> *Isaiah 59:1-2 [NKJV]*
> *1 Behold, the LORD's hand is not shortened, that it cannot save; nor His ear heavy, that it cannot hear.*
> *2 But your iniquities have separated you from your God; and your sins have hidden His face from you, So that He will not hear.*

In chapter four of this book, I write about the importance of prayer. However, I will want you to know that the vessel conducting or saying a prayer is more important than the prayer that is been said. Why is this so? Let's find out in God's Word. The Bible tells us that God does not hear the prayer of a sinner.

> *John 9:31 [NKJV]*
> *Now we know that God does not hear sinners; but if anyone is a worshiper of God and does His will, He hears him.*

> *Proverbs 15:8 [NKJV]*
> *The sacrifice of the wicked is an abomination to the LORD, but the prayer of the upright is His delight.*

The exception to the above Scriptures is the sinner's prayer of repentance and forgiveness. Now who is a sinner? A sinner is any person who is yet to experience the new birth by making Jesus Lord of his or her life [that is; born again, *John 3:3*]. The new birth brings the new life from God's Holy Spirit, and this new life always reflects God's Word [the Bible]. In the preface of this book, I wrote about how one can receive the new birth. As Christians, when our doings run contrary to God's Word, our salvation experience becomes questionable.

~

"When we pray to God according to His Word, our prayers are supposed to move the hands of God to act on our behalf and produce the desired results."

The prayer of a sinner can be counterproductive. The Bible tells us about seven men who in an attempt to cast out demons from one man, got seriously beaten up by the one man possessed by the demons. The beating received by these seven men was so much that they went home naked and bleeding. See Scripture reference below:

Acts 19:13-16 [NIV]
13 Some Jews who went around driving out evil spirits tried to invoke the name of the Lord Jesus over those who were demon-possessed. They would say, "In the name of Jesus, whom Paul preaches, I command you to come out."
14 Seven sons of Sceva, a Jewish chief priest, were doing this.
15 (One day) the evil spirit answered them, "Jesus I

know, and I know about Paul, but who are you?"
16 Then the man who had the evil spirit jumped on
them and overpowered them all. He gave them such
a beating that they ran out of the house naked and
bleeding.

From the above Bible verses, it is seen that the seven men who got beaten were not believing Christians [born again] because they prayed in the Name of Jesus whom Paul preaches, showing clearly that they themselves had no relationship and fellowship with the Name of Jesus.

A great lesson to learn from the above verses is that you cannot borrow the Name of Jesus for use and later dump it. There are people who pray to God, or go to church only when they are in serious need. You must have a relationship and be in constant fellowship with Jesus for you to be able to pray effectively in His Name. In the secular world, people borrow things that they don't have, use them for a short time and later return the borrowed items back to the owner. Now you can see that this cannot be done with the Name of Jesus.

The story of the seven sons of Sceva shows clearly that the person praying is more important than the prayer it-self. Their problem was not the Name of Jesus because the demons identified Jesus' Name. They even identified Paul's name too. As concerning Jesus and Paul, they said, *"Jesus I know, and Paul I know,"* but as for the seven sons of Sceva, they said *"but who are you?"* My dear reader, I have the same question for you;—who are you?

The Bible tells us that it is the prayer of a righteous man that makes tremendous power available. It is not just the prayer of any man, but the prayer of a righteous man. See Scripture reference below:

James 5:16 [AMP]
Confess to one another therefore your faults (your slips, your false steps, your offenses, your sins) and pray [also] for one another, that you may be healed and restored [to a spiritual tone of mind and heart]. The earnest (heartfelt, continued) ***prayer of a righteous man makes tremendous power available*** *[dynamic in its working].*

The Bible verse above reiterates the importance of the praying vessel over the prayer being said. The vessel should first confess his or her sins before saying the prayer so that the prayer is not hindered. Note that this verse is addressing believers who may have sinned as a result of engaging themselves in acts contrary to God's Word.

The importance of the person saying the prayer can be seen clearly in *2 Chronicles 7:14;*

2 Chronicles 7:14 [KJV]
If My people who are called by My name *will humble themselves, and pray and seek My face, and turn from their wicked ways, then I will hear from heaven, and will forgive their sin and heal their land.*

~

"You must have a relationship and be in constant fellowship with Jesus for you to be able to pray effectively in His Name."

We can see again from this Scripture, that apart from the prayer, the person saying the prayer has to be in line with God and His Word. The words in bold in that verse *"if my people who are called by my name"* are referring to the person saying the prayer. This verse of Scripture talks about four specific things that are required in order for our prayers to receive speedy answers from God. These four things are: Called by God's Name, humble one's self, seek God's face, and turn from wicked ways. These four are expounded below.

■ 1. Called by God's Name

Called by God's Name can be said to mean surnamed God. This means: the person is related to God or belongs to God's family. Accepting Jesus as Lord and Savior is the only way to become a member of God's family. As stated in *Romans 8:16-17*, those who have accepted Jesus as Lord and Savior are heirs of God the Father, joint heirs with Jesus the Son, and are called children of God's Kingdom.

■ 2. Humble one's self

The Bible tells us in *James 4:6* that God resists the proud in spirit, but gives much grace to the humble. Gives grace to the humble, means unmerited favor. That is; as the humble in spirit prays to God, his or her prayers get answers because the person is in favor with God. Our prayers are unproductive in the presence of pride. Pride is a strong hindrance to our prayers because it puts us at odds with God [because God resists the proud]. See the parable below Jesus gave about a man who prayed with pride in heart.

Luke 18:10-14 [NKJV]
10 Two men went up to the temple to pray, one a Pharisee and the other a tax collector.
11 The Pharisee stood and prayed thus with himself, 'God, I thank You that I am not like other men, extortioners, unjust, adulterers, or even as this tax collector.
12 I fast twice a week; I give tithes of all that I possess.
13 And the tax collector, standing afar off, would not so much as raise his eyes to heaven, but beat his breast, saying, 'God, be merciful to me a sinner!
14 I tell you, this man went down to his house justified rather than the other; for everyone who exalts himself will be humbled, and he who humbles himself will be exalted.

From the above Scriptures, you can see that the prayer of the humble person [tax collector] got a speedy answer, while that of the Pharisee was not answered. Note: that the Pharisee prayed in faith; however, because of the presence of pride, he was not justified. Also, we can see that the Pharisee prayed wrongly because of his pride. Though he started by thanking God [*verse 11*], he went off track by comparing himself with others and even talking them down before God which is not in line with God's Word because the Bible tells us that people who compare themselves with others are not wise, *2 Corinthians 10:12*.

The above Scripture of *Luke 18:10-14*, also teaches us that being religious or born into a religious family does not mean automatic answers to prayers. There must be a personal relationship with Jesus. The Pharisees are known to be very religious and hold to their religious believes rather than the finished work of grace. I have met people who always acclaim to be of the Christian faith because they are from Christian families. Being born into a Christian family is good, because one will be nurtured after the ways of God, however it is not what brings salvation or opens the doors of Heaven to our prayers, rather our personal relationship and fellowship with the Lord Jesus that gives the access to God.

■ 3. Seek God's face

The praying believer should seek God's face by studying God's Word [the Bible]; God's will is revealed in His Word. This is important because a shallow or zero knowledge of God can cause a believer to attempt to seek God through the wrong medium. Going through the wrong medium, leads one to destruction and untimely death. This was the case of King Saul who contracted the service of demonic spiritualist [witch or wizard], *1 Samuel 28:7*.

The Bible tells us in *Deuteronomy 18:9-12* not to seek help from palm readers and spiritualists conjuring with familiar spirits of the dead and to desist from reading or conjuring witchcraft books of divination. The *Book of Isaiah 8:19* admonishes us to seek God's face and not to go after necromancers [those who conjure with the dead]. If for any reason you had conjured or presently conjuring with any of the satanic mediums mentioned above, it is of vital importance that you repent immediately and seek the help of a Bible base deliverance minister for counseling and deliverance.

~

"A shallow or zero knowledge of God can cause a believer to attempt to seek God through the wrong medium."

■ 4. Turn from wicked ways

Wickedness is disobeying God and His Word. The praying vessel should turn from sinful wicked ways and surrender totally to God for forgiveness because the prayers [sacrifices] of the wicked are an abomination to God, *Proverbs 15:8.*

> *Proverbs 15:8 [NKJV]*
> *The sacrifice of the wicked is an abomination to the LORD, but the prayer of the upright is His delight.*

Strategic Prayer Points and Declarations

STRATEGIC PRAYER

■ 1. Pray that the spirit of apostasy; renouncing and forsaking of the Christian faith and belief never come on you. *1 Timothy 4:1 (NKJV) "Now the Spirit expressly says that in latter times some will depart from the faith, giving heed to deceiving spirits and doctrines of demons"*

■ 2. Pray that the demonic spirit of pride never finds a place in your heart and that you be enveloped with God's Spirit of grace and humility daily in Jesus' Name. *Proverbs 16:18 (NKJV) "Pride goes before destruction, and a haughty spirit before a fall"*

■ 3. Pray against the spirit of timidity [fear, intimidation] in believing Christians and that God grant unto them boldness to preach Jesus to the unsaved everywhere in the world, *[2 Timothy 1:7, Acts 4:14, 29, 31].*

■ 4. Pray against the spirit of unbelief that acts as a short circuit to the flow of God's Word in the heart of people thereby preventing the work of God from making advancement, *[Matthew 13:58].*

■ 5. Pray against falling away [backsliding] and for those who have backslidden because of unbelief, to be restored back to glory, *[Hebrews 3:12]*

STRATEGIC DECLARATIONS

■ 1. Father God I declare by your grace that I shall not renounce Jesus or my faith in Jesus Christ. I will endure to the end in Jesus' Name, Amen. *Matthew 24:13 (NKJV)* *"But he who endures to the end shall be saved"*

■ 2. Father God I receive grace from You continually to advance and ultimately finish the course set before me. *2 Timothy 4:7 (NKJV) "I have fought the good fight, I have finished the race, I have kept the faith"*

■ 3. Father God I declare that pride will not be lifted in my heart and I will be clothed with humility in Jesus' Name, *James 4:6.*

■ 4. I receive grace to continually manifest the fruit of the Holy Spirit in my life daily in Jesus' Name, Amen. *(James 4:6)*

∼

Chapter 4
Importance of Prayer

The importance of prayer to a Christian cannot be over-emphasized. Through prayer, the believer's joy overflows. Jesus said in *John 16:24 "Until now you have asked nothing in My name. Ask, and you will receive, that your joy may be full."* It is wonderful to know that when we ask in prayer, we receive and our joy overflows. But let's take a closer look at the above Scripture. It says until now you have asked nothing in my Name; this means that Jesus was concerned about the disciples lack of asking in prayer and He [Jesus] never wanted them to stay in that condition; hence He [Jesus] instructed them to ask so that their joy would be full.

Prayer is needed by believers for them to be an effective weapon in God's hand. Oh yes—a weapon in God's hand. Now this may sound strange to you if you are hearing it for the first time. Anyway, you are not alone, because many others find it difficult to comprehend that they are the weapons God uses in the battle front for His will to be executed here on Earth. The Bible tells us that we are God's weapons of war.

Jeremiah 51:20-23 [KJV]
20 Thou art my battle-axe and weapons of war: for with thee will I break in pieces the nations, and with thee will I destroy kingdoms;
21 And with thee will I break in pieces the horse and his rider; and with thee will I break in pieces the chariot and his rider;
22 With thee also will I break in pieces man and woman; and with thee will I break in pieces old and young; and with thee will I break in pieces the young man and the maid;
23 I will also break in pieces with thee the shepherd and his flock; and with thee will I break in pieces the husbandman and his yoke of oxen; and with thee will I break in pieces captains and rulers.

The above Scripture reference not only tells us that we are God's weapons of war, it also says that with us He will execute His desired will here on Earth; like pulling down satanic kingdoms, strongholds, and releasing healing in the land, *2 Chronicles 7:14.*

~

"Prayer is needed by believers for them to be an effective weapon in God's hand."

Prayer is the medium by which believers unleash God's heavenly will upon the earth. While teaching His disciples how to pray, Jesus asked them to pray for God's heavenly will to be carried out here on Earth;

> *Luke 11:2 [NKJV]*
> *So He said to them, "When you pray, say: Our Father*
> *in heaven, Hallowed be Your name. Your kingdom*
> *come. Your will be done On earth as it is in heaven.*

The above Bible verse reminds us about God's love and interest for us here on Earth. It is God's desire that His will be carried out here on Earth. But you see; this desire of our heavenly Father can only be released through believer's prayers. The Word of God tells us in *Matthew 18:18* that Heaven acts or gets into full action only when we first act and get into action here on Earth—through our prayers.

> *Matthew 18:18 [NKJV]*
> *Assuredly, I say to you, whatever you bind on earth*
> *will be bound in heaven, and whatever you loose on*
> *earth will be loosed in heaven.*

From the above Scripture reference, we can rightfully say that: Heaven does nothing until we do something here on Earth. This means that our prayer here on Earth is what moves God to act. Simply put "as touching what goes on here on Earth, whatever we say or permit in our prayers that are in line with God's Word—Heaven agrees." This means if we shut our mouth in prayer, we are shutting Heaven's gates and windows and allowing Satan and his demons to control the affairs of the earth. But when we open our mouth in prayer and pray strategically according to God's Word, we keep the gates and windows of Heaven open for God's will to be unleashed on Earth and disallow the works of Satan and his demons.

~

"Heaven acts or gets into full action only when we first act and get into action here on Earth—through our prayers."

Does this means we take the lead in deciding what goes on here on Earth? Well; the answer is simply yes from the two Scriptures above. Now this may be hard for some of us to accept because we are always waiting for God to act or do something without us doing anything because we feel the responsibility is God's. Well the responsibility is not God's, rather it is ours because He has given us the authority to rule and dominate in the earth. Let me take your mind back to the time of creation in *Genesis 1:26*;

> *Genesis 1:26 [NKJV]*
> *Then God said, "Let Us make man in Our image, according to Our likeness; let them have dominion over the fish of the sea, over the birds of the air, and over the cattle, over all the earth and over every creeping thing that creeps on the earth."*

The above Scripture verse clearly shows that after God created man, He gave man the authority to rule over the earth and everything contained in it. Take note of the fact that God said, *"let them have dominion over,"* and not *"let us have dominion over."* Let us means that God and man have dominion over Earth. But let them means man alone (man and woman) created by God is given the authority to dominate Earth.

After the fall of man, God's plan of redemption through His Son Jesus restored man back to the position of authority to dominate over the earth. God's work of redemption for man was accomplished through the death, burial and resurrection of our Lord Jesus. Jesus declared this completed work on the cross by saying—it is finished.

John 19:30 [KJV]
When Jesus therefore had received the vinegar, he said, It is finished: and he bowed his head, and gave up the ghost.

The same Jesus Who declared it finished has bequeathed this finished work to us. So it is up to us to declare and release the finished work of God over the nations and kingdoms of the earth through our prayers. The Bible tells us in the *Book of John 14:12-14.*

John 14:12-14 [NKJV]
12 Most assuredly, I say to you, he who believes in Me, the works that I do he will do also; and greater works than these he will do, because I go to My Father.
13 And whatever you ask in My name, that I will do, that the Father may be glorified in the Son.

14 If you ask anything in My name, I will do it.

In verse twelve to fourteen above, Jesus is speaking pro-phetically of what will be. *"The works that I do, he will do and even greater works because I go to my father, and whatever you ask in my name, I will do"* means; He [Jesus] bequeathed the finished work to us because He would no longer be here, all we need to do to get the same work and greater works done on Earth (so His [Jesus] will contin-ues), is to ask [pray to Father God] in His [Jesus'] Name.

The story Jesus gave about a widow in *Luke 18:1-8* under-scores the importance of prayer. Jesus said in verse one, that believers are supposed to be engaged constantly in prayer and not to faint. Using the example of the widow who got her victory because she troubled the judge in charge of her case every day, Jesus said when believers pray to God con-tinuously about any issue, they will for sure get the answer from Father God. Even on issues that have lingered for a long time, Jesus said continuous daily prayers would move God to act quickly. See Scripture reference below.

> *Luke 18:7-8 [AMP]*
> *7 And will not [our just] God defend and protect and avenge His elect (His chosen ones), who cry to Him day and night? Will He defer them and delay help on their behalf?*
> *8 I tell you, He will defend and protect and avenge them speedily. However, when the Son of Man comes, will He find [persistence in] faith on the earth?*

Strategic Prayer Points and Declarations

STRATEGIC PRAYER

■ 1. Pray against lying spirits that has invaded the world with wrong teachings that says, "prayer is no more necessary." Prayer is the core of the Christian faith as Jesus said in *Luke 18:1 [NIV] Then Jesus told his disciples a parable to show them that they should always pray and not give up.*

■ 2. Prayer for the spiritual understanding of believers to be enlightened as regarding the importance of prayer in the Church and Christian ministry, *2 Corinthians 4:4.*

■ 3. Pray that you will be fruitful in the place of prayer, producing God's desired results.

STRATEGIC DECLARATIONS

■ 1. I give myself to prayer and to the study of the Word of God. *Acts 6:4 [NKJV] but we will give ourselves continually to prayer and to the ministry of the word.*

■ 2. I refuse to be on and off in my prayer life. I receive grace from the Lord to pray on regular basis (praying without ceasing), *1 Thessalonians 5:17 [NKJV] pray without ceasing.*

■ 3. Slothfulness will not be found in me, I will be fervent in the spirit in my service to the Lord in Jesus' Name. *Romans 12:11 [KJV] Not slothful in business; fervent in spirit; serving the Lord.*

∽

Chapter 5

God is Looking for Praying Believers

God is constantly on the look for believers who are strategically positioned and prepared for Him. God is looking for praying believers [intercessors] to stand in the gap and be the medium by which He [God] will execute His will on Earth. In *Ezekiel 22:29-31* God consumed a wicked nation because He could not find a praying person to stand in the gap to intercede for the people to be delivered. [See Scripture reference below]

> *Ezekiel 22:29-31 [KJV]*
> *29 The people of the land have used oppression, and exercised robbery, and have vexed the poor and needy: yea, they have oppressed the stranger wrongfully.*
> *30 **And I sought for a man among them**, that should make up the hedge, and stand in the gap before me for the land, that I should not destroy it: but I found none.*
> *31 Therefore have I poured out mine indignation upon them; I have consumed them with the fire of my wrath: their own way have I recompensed upon their heads, saith the Lord GOD.*

The bold sentence in verse thirty above means God sought for an intercessor among the people who will stand between the people and God and intercede [pray] for their salvation but God found none. If God had found a praying believer to stand in the gap and intercede for the people, He would have had mercy and forgive their sins and healed their land.

~

"God is looking for praying believers [intercessors] to stand in the gap and be the medium by which He [God] will execute His will on Earth."

No matter how bad the situation might be, even to the extent of God being against a person, family, city, nation, kingdom, etc. (because of their sins and abominations); if God can find a compassionate praying Christian, He [God] will have mercy, forgive and heal their land. In the Book of *2 Chronicles 7:13-14*, God said that if He finds praying believers who will pray and turn from their wicked ways, He will have mercy and heal their land of the destruction He [God] allowed on them because of their sins;

> *2 Chronicles 7:13-14 [KJV]*
> *13 If I shut up heaven that there be no rain, or if I command the locusts to devour the land, or if I send pestilence among my people;*

*14 **If my people, which are called by my name, shall humble themselves, and pray, and seek my face, and turn from their wicked ways;** then will I hear from heaven, and will forgive their sin, and will heal their land.*

Verse fourteen above implies that God is looking for praying men and women, who will pray for their land to advert impending destruction. If our prayers can make God change His mind and forgive nations and kingdoms of the sins they have committed and heal their land, then guess what? Our prayers can cause the maximum havoc you can ever think of in the kingdom of darkness.

God is constantly appointing praying believers to pray over nations for His will to be done on the earth. In *Isaiah 62:6-7*, God appointed prayer warriors [intercessor], to pray for Jerusalem until Jerusalem becomes a center of praise.

> *Isaiah 62:6-7 [NKJV]*
> *6 I have set watchmen on your walls, O Jerusalem; They shall never hold their peace day or night. You who make mention of the Lord, do not keep silent,*
> *7 And give Him no rest till He establishes And till He makes Jerusalem a praise in the earth.*

The above Scripture in verse six can be said to mean that God is constantly recruiting and strategically positioning His children to intercede for nations all over the world.

If you are an intercessor, know from today that you were recruited and strategically positioned by God and not by yourself. Therefore, carry out your intercessor assignment with all your heart and might because God Who recruited you requires you to be faithful. *1 Corinthians 4:2* tells us that; it is a requirement in stewardship that one be faithful.

The Bible recorded various instances indicating the need for praying believers in the body of Christ. Below are a few of them.

Jesus requesting for prayers at the garden of Gethsemane

At the garden of Gethsemane, Jesus requested His disciples to watch with Him in prayer for one hour. This was at the toughest moment where His soul was sorrowful unto death. Now Jesus can pray alone because He doesn't need the prayers of His disciples for Him to be able to go through the sorrowful moment. But for His disciples not to enter temptation, He asked them to join Him in prayer.

> *Matthew 26:40-41 [NKJV]*
> *40 Then He came to the disciples and found them sleeping, and said to Peter, "What! Could you not watch with Me one hour?*
> *41 Watch and pray, lest you enter into temptation. The spirit indeed is willing, but the flesh is weak."*

Verse forty above, reminds us that we are required to pray

for our loved ones whenever they are going through the toughest moment of their life and not to gossip and talk them down because of what they are going through.

~

"God is constantly recruiting and strategically positioning His children to intercede for nations all over the world."

Jesus requesting prayers for more laborers

Jesus requested His disciples to pray for more laborers for the huge work of the ministry.

> *Luke 10:2 [NKJV]*
> *Then He said to them, "The harvest truly is great, but the laborers are few; therefore pray the Lord of the harvest to send out laborers into His harvest.*

The request to pray for more laborers was because of few laborers; few prayer warriors, few evangelists, few teachers etc. This tells us that God is looking for praying believers to position them over nations for the huge work of the ministry.

The Apostles giving themselves to prayer

In *Acts 6:1-4*, when the apostles were faced with care issues because of the explosive growth of the ministry, they appointed deacons to oversee and care for the welfare of the brethren. But they dedicated themselves to prayer and the Word. See Scripture reference below.

Acts 6:1-4 [NKJV]
1Now in those days, when the number of the disciples was multiplying, there arose a complaint against the Hebrews by the Hellenists, because their widows were neglected in the daily distribution.
2 Then the twelve summoned the multitude of the disciples and said, "It is not desirable that we should leave the word of God and serve tables.
3 Therefore, brethren, seek out from among you seven men of good reputation, full of the Holy Spirit and wisdom, whom we may appoint over this business;
*4 **But we will give ourselves continually to prayer and to the ministry of the word.**"*

The above Scripture verses clearly tell us that prayer and the Word should not be placed behind or take the back seat as it is today in many ministries and churches, rather it should take the lead and be in the forefront. Today many ministries spend more time in social activities than in prayer. As important as social activities are, they should not replace or eat into the times of prayer in a ministry or church. When you call for a fasting and prayer meeting, the attendance is usually very low as compared to when you call for a social gathering. This is not supposed to be so; rather we should give ourselves more to prayer than social activities; as the apostles did in their time.

Jesus declaring the temple a place of prayer

It is a painful thing that the Church today has been turned from what Jesus who founded and built it intended it to be *[Matthew 16:18 "...I will build my church and the gates of hell will not overcome it"]*. The Church is now luke-warm in the aspect of prayers, *Revelations 3:16*. This was the case in the time of Jesus when the temple was turned from what God intended it into a place of trading, money making, and fun. See Scripture reference below.

Mark 11:17 [NKJV]
Then He taught, saying to them, "Is it not written, 'My house shall be called a house of prayer for all na-tions'? But you have made it a 'den of thieves.

~

"Today many ministries spend more time in social activities than in prayer."

Today people see church primarily as a place where you connect with other people. Some even see it as a place to socialize and start physical relationship with others instead of a spiritual relationship and growth with the Lord Jesus. Connecting with people is a lovely thing and should be encouraged if it is done right according to the Word of God. However, it should not be the primary rea-son we go to church.

Strategic Prayer Points and Declarations

STRATEGIC PRAYER

■ 1. Pray that God will raise up praying believers who will stand in the gap through prayer to declare God's will over nations, kingdoms, government etc., so that we can live peaceably. *Isaiah 62:6 [NKJV] I have set watchmen on your walls, O Jerusalem; They shall never hold their peace day or night. You who make mention of the Lord, do not keep silent.*

■ 2. Pray for the revitalization of believers who are weak in the place of prayer and fasting. *Isaiah 40:29 [NKJV] He gives power to the weak, and to those who have no might He increases strength.*

■ 3. Pray that your loved ones and people where you are located will heed to the Gospel of Christ, turn from their wicked ways and begin to seek God's plan for their life, *2 Chronicles 7:14.*

STRATEGIC DECLARATIONS

■ 1. As a believing Christian, I belong to the army of God, commissioned by Jesus Himself as written in *Mark 16:17.*

■ 2. I refuse to be weak in the place of prayer, I receive grace to be more effective in praying in Jesus' Name. *2 Corinthians 12:9 [NKJV] And He said to me, "My grace is sufficient for you, for My strength is made perfect in weakness.*

■ 3. My past cannot dictate my present and my future because whatever wrong I did before I accepted Jesus has been wiped out by Jesus. *Colossians 2:14 [NKJV] having wiped out the handwriting of requirements that was against us, which was contrary to us. And He has taken it out of the way, having nailed it to the cross.*

~

Chapter 6
Know Why You are Praying

Many pray without knowing why they are praying. Praying without knowing why is like a man travelling without knowing why. Such a journey always ends fruitless. Our prayers become misguided and fruitless when we don't know why we are praying. Misguided prayers are prayers that end up being done for the wrong purpose [amiss] and selfish motives for sensual or fleshly pleasures [lusts]. See underline italics in the Scripture references below, *James 4:3.*

> *James 4:3 [AMP]*
> *[Or] you do ask [God for them] and yet fail to receive, because <u>you ask with wrong purpose and evil, selfish motives.</u> Your intention is [when you get what you desire] to spend it in sensual pleasures.*

> *James 4:3 [KJV]*
> *Ye ask, and receive not, <u>because ye ask amiss,</u> that ye may consume it upon your lusts.*

Let's revisit the Bible *Book of Ephesians 6:12* because it clearly points us to why we pray. See Scripture below.

Ephesians 6:12 [NKJV]
For we do not wrestle against flesh and blood, but
against principalities, against powers, against the
rulers of the darkness of this age, against spiritual
hosts of wickedness in the heavenly places.

Ephesians 6:12 clearly says that we fight against spiritual wicked forces [satan and his demons] in heavenly places. Now this is a great revelation because you cannot fight spirits with physical weapons. Rather you fight spiritual forces with spiritual weapons. As I explain in chapter one of this book, prayer is a key spiritual weapon used to deploy God's spiritual armor listed in the Bible *Book of Ephesians 6:14-17.*

~

"Our prayers become misguided and fruitless when we don't know why we are praying."

When we pray without knowing why, we are simply demonstrating our ignorance of God's Word. Let's see some biblical examples of peoples that got results because they knew why they had to pray:

Nehemiah's Prayer

Nehemiah prayed because the city of Jerusalem laid waste, the walls were broken down and the people that were left of the captivity were in great danger and terrible affliction.

Nehemiah 1:3-4 [NKJV]
3 And they said to me, "The survivors who are left
from the captivity in the province are there in great
distress and reproach. The wall of Jerusalem is also
broken down, and its gates are burned with fire."
4 So it was, when I heard these words that I sat down
and wept, and mourned for many days; I was fasting
and praying before the God of heaven.

What triggered Nehemiah's prayer was the condition of
his brethren and the city of Jerusalem. He knew why he
had to pray and his prayer was answered because the city
was rebuilt. Praise God. [See the entire *Book of Nehemiah* in the Bible].

The Prayer of the Apostles

In *Acts 4:29*, the apostles prayed because they were being threatened by the chief priests and elders because of a
notable miracle performed by the apostles that is clearly
manifested and seen by all *(Acts 3: 1-10; 4:14-18)*.

Acts 4:17,29, 31 [NKJV]
*17 But so that it spreads no further among the peo-
ple, let us severely threaten them, that from now on*
they speak to no man in this name.
29 Now, Lord, look on their threats, and grant to Your
servants that with all boldness they may speak Your word.
31 And when they had prayed, the place where they
were assembled together was shaken; and they were

all filled with the Holy Spirit, and they spoke the word of God with boldness.

We must know why we pray when we are called to pray. No matter the kind of prayer we are embarked upon; intercessory, thanksgiving, consecration, warfare etc., we must know why we are praying. Because the apostles knew why they were praying, their prayers generated enough power to the extent that the place they were assembled was shaken.

~

"You cannot fight spirits with physical weapons. Rather you fight spiritual forces with spiritual weapons."

The prayer of Esther

Esther, a Jew declared a three-day fasting and prayer when her nation was faced with a genocidal plan from Haman who is a right-hand man of the king of his time. This is recorded in the Bible *Book of Esther* chapter three and four. Esther fasted and prayed to expose and stop Haman's genocidal plan. Her prayer worked because she knew why she had to pray. Haman was not only stopped, but his wicked plan was turned on him.

Hezekiah's prayer

Hezekiah prayed because he was sick to the point of death

and in addition to his sickness, he got an unpleasant message from God's prophet Isaiah that he will surely die, *2 Kings 20:1-5*. His prayer was answered because he knew why he had to pray. He got restored and God added fifteen more years to him. See Scripture below.

2 Kings 20:1-5 [NKJV]
1 In those days Hezekiah was sick and near death. And Isaiah the prophet, the son of Amoz, went to him and said to him, "Thus says the Lord: 'Set your house in order, for you shall die, and not live.
2 Then he turned his face toward the wall, and prayed to the Lord, saying,
3 Remember now, O Lord, I pray, how I have walked before You in truth and with a loyal heart, and have done what was good in Your sight." And Hezekiah wept bitterly.
4 And it happened, before Isaiah had gone out into the middle court, that the word of the Lord came to him, saying,
5 Return and tell Hezekiah the leader of My people, 'Thus says the Lord, the God of David your father: "I have heard your prayer, I have seen your tears; surely I will heal you. On the third day you shall go up to the house of the Lord.
6 And I will add to your days fifteen years. I will deliver you and this city from the hand of the king of Assyria; and I will defend this city for My own sake, and for the sake of My servant David.

Strategic Prayer Points and Declarations

STRATEGIC PRAYER

■ 1. Pray that God will grant you and your loved one's justice against all your adversaries in Jesus' Name. *Luke 18:3 [NIV] ...Grant me justice against my adversary.*

■ 2. Pray for God to turn around every negative report or evil plan for your good and the good of your loved ones in Jesus' Name. *Genesis 50:20 [NKJV] But as for you, you meant evil against me; but God meant it for good, in order to bring it about as it is this day, to save many people alive.*

■ 3. Pray that every evil plan towards you and your loved ones will boomerang on the originator of the evil plan. *Proverbs 26:27 [NKJV] Whoever digs a pit will fall into it, and he who rolls a stone will have it roll back on him.*

STRATEGIC DECLARATIONS

■ 1. I will not fail, faint, fall, or be weary in all my endeavors because my hope and trust is in the Lord. *Isaiah 40:30-31 [NIV] 30 Even youths grow tired and weary, and young men stumble and fall; 31 but those who hope in the Lord will renew their strength They will soar on wings like eagles; they will run and not grow weary, they will walk and not be faint.*

■ 2. By the grace of God, I am rich. I cannot be poor because Jesus became poor that through His poverty I might be rich. Therefore, I reject every poverty mentality and mindset in Jesus' Name. *2 Corinthians 8:9 [NKJV] For you know the grace of our Lord Jesus Christ, that though He was rich, yet for your sakes He became poor, that you through His poverty might become rich.*

■ 3. As written in *Romans 1:17, the just shall live by faith.* As a result, I refuse to live in fear of any kind in Jesus' Name.

~

Chapter 7
Know What You are Praying For

Many believers in the body of Christ pray regularly, but only few believers pray strategically, that is; know what they are praying for and launch their prayer on target. Some time ago, a sister approached me to agree with her in prayer concerning a poor decision she has just made in purchasing a car. In presenting her situation to me she used the following words;

> *"Pastor, I just made a poor decision by signing documents for a car and do not know what to do, in fact I am confused about the situation...I did not thoroughly read the documents before signing...I don't know if I should pick up the car or not.... I am just confused, please pastor pray for me."*

After listening to her, I knew why to pray (which is; for her confused state of mind), but I do not know what to pray for. Now if I pray for her not to be confused, she will leave happily but the prayer will not work because the root cause of the confusion, which is; the poor decision in signing a car document without reviewing the details is still there. Rather I asked her what specifically she wanted me to pray for. Now, because of her confused mind, she simply replied pastor I don't know. Then I helped her by giving her the following options:

▶ 1. Do you want the dealer to reduce the price to what you like, and you pick the car? Or

▶ 2. Do you want the deal to be cancelled without any liability to you?

She thought about both options for a short moment and then picked number two. Then I said all right we have something to pray about. I held her hand in agreement and prayed the prayer of agreement using God's Word in *Matthew 18:19*.

In most of the miracles performed by Jesus, He asked the recipients what specifically He should do for them. This can be seen in the miracle He performed for the two blind men, Jesus asked them *"what do you want me to do for you?"* even when He [Jesus] knew that they were blind. See Scripture reference below.

> *Matthew 20:30, 32 [NKJV]*
> *30 And behold, two blind men sitting by the road, when they heard that Jesus was passing by, cried out, saying, "Have mercy on us, O Lord, Son of David!"*
> *32 So Jesus stood still and called them, and said, "What do you want Me to do for you?"*

People usually have this misconception: that because God knows their problem, they are not to be specific about what the issue is when praying to God. In fact, some will say they don't need to pray at all because God already knows what their need is. This is misleading because it has no scriptural backing.

~

"Few believers pray strategically, that is; know what they are praying for and launch their prayer on target."

What you are praying for can be confused with why you are praying because they sound similar and appear to have the same meaning. Let's review some biblical examples.

Prayer of Hannah

1 Samuel 1: 6, 10-11 [KJV]
6 And her rival also provoked her severely, to make her miserable, because the Lord had closed her womb.
10 And she was in bitterness of soul, and prayed to the Lord and wept in anguish.
11 Then she made a vow and said, "O Lord of hosts, if You will indeed look on the affliction of Your maidservant and remember me, and not forget Your maidservant, but will give Your maidservant a male child, then I will give him to the Lord all the days of his life, and no razor shall come upon his head."

The underlined in *verse 11* above is what Hannah prayed for [for God to give her a male child], which is different from the reason why she prayed [barren, afflicted and being provoked by her adversary, *verse 6*]. Knowing why we pray without knowing what to pray for may make our prayers unanswered. Knowing what to pray is the next step after knowing why to pray.

Prayer of Jesus for Unity

John 17:20-21 [NKJV]
20 "I do not pray for these alone, but also for those who will believe in Me through their word; 21 <u>that they all may be one</u>, as You, Father, are in Me, and I in You; that they also may be one in Us, <u>that the world may believe that You sent Me.</u>

The first underline in verse 21 above is what Jesus prayed for *"that they all may be one,"* while the second underlined *"that the world may believe that You sent Me"* is the why he prayed.

Below is hypothetical prayer illustration of a homeless person.

Hypothetical homeless situation prayer illustration:

■ 1. Father God this homeless situation I am in, has affected my ability to function to the fullness of the potential You have deposited in me, I pray that You have mercy on me.

■ 2. Father God this homeless situation I am in has affected my ability to function to the fullness of the potential You have deposited in me, I pray that You have mercy on me, take me out of this predicament by providing me my own apartment in Jesus' Name.

Now if I stop at the first prayer point, my prayer is inconclusive because, I know why I am praying, but I don't know what to pray about to address why I am praying. But the second prayer point brings **"what I am praying for"** into the picture [provide me my own apartment]. This is exactly how Hannah handled her prayer by reminding God of her being provoked because she was barren, and she prayed for God to give her a man-child. And not only that, she went further to vow a vow unto God on why she needed a man child.

$\sim$

"In most of the miracles performed by Jesus, He asked the recipients what specifically He should do for them."

The prayer of Jabez

Jabez's prayer is among the strategic prayers listed in the Bible.

1 Chronicles 4:10 [NKJV]
And Jabez called on the God of Israel saying,

"Oh, that You would bless me indeed, and enlarge my territory, that Your hand would be with me, and that You would keep me from evil, that I may not cause pain!" So God granted him what he requested.

Knowing what to pray for is clearly seen in the prayer of Jabez as seen in the Scripture above. Jabez listed the specific things he wanted God to do for him and God granted his request. The what we pray for brings out the specifics of our prayers.

Strategic Prayer Points and Declarations

STRATEGIC PRAYER

■ 1. Receive prosperity in your life by praying for the peace of Jerusalem. *Psalms 122:6 [NKJV] Pray for the peace of Jerusalem: "May they prosper who love you.*

■ 2. Pray the below Jabez prayer points in *1 Chronicles 4:10* over your life and loved ones.

• Father God bless me and my loved ones in Jesus' Name

• Father God enlarge my territory (business, ministry etc.) in Jesus' Name

• Father God keep me from evil in Jesus' Name.

• Father God let your hand always be with me and guide

me in Jesus' Name.

• Father God pilot my life and the life of my loved ones so that we will not cause pain to people and society in Jesus' Name.

■ 3. Pray that all forms of bareness in your life and loved ones cease and that God will make you productive, fruitful and fulfilled as He has said in His Word concerning you. *Exodus 23:26 [NKJV] No one shall suffer miscarriage or be barren in your land; I will fulfill the number of your days.*

STRATEGIC DECLARATIONS

■ 1. According to the Word of God in *Isaiah 62:1,* my righteousness shall shine like the dawn therefore I refuse to allow darkness rule in my territory in Jesus' Name.

■ 2. Evil will not come near me and my loved ones in Jesus' Name because according to the Word of God in *Psalms 91:7 [NKJV], a thousand may fall at your side, and ten thousand at your right hand; but it shall not come near you.*

■ 3. I am divinely protected in Jesus and as such I am not afraid of day time or night time terror. *Psalms 91:5 [NKJV] You shall not be afraid of the terror by night, nor of the arrow that flies by day.*

~

Chapter 8
Know How to Pray – Part One

Not knowing how to pray can either make us not to pray or pray wrongly. I have seen people who have been Christians for years not knowing how to pray when called to say a simple prayer during a prayer session. If you are in this category, don't feel bad because Jesus disciples once find themselves in the same situation. Seeing Jesus praying, the disciples became eager to learn how to pray that they asked Jesus saying; Lord teach us how to pray.

> *Luke 11:1 [KJV]*
> *And it came to pass, that, as he was praying in a certain place, when he ceased, one of his disciples said unto him, Lord, teach us to pray, as John also taught his disciples.*

Note that it was one of the disciples that asked Jesus to teach them how to pray. This means that disciple had the desire to pray, but his problem was the how to pray. The eagerness and thirst of praying precedes the how of praying. You must first love prayer or praying before you can learn how to pray. For example; those who hate driving finds it difficult to learn how to drive.

Prayer and the Holy Spirit

Our prayer know how rests on the Holy Spirit. Just as Jesus disciples ask Him to teach them how to pray, believers should constantly ask the Holy Spirit to teach them how to pray using God's Word. We cannot learn or master any spiritual warfare without the help of the Holy Spirit, because it is the Holy Spirit that will teach us all things;

John 14:26 [AMP]
*But the Comforter (Counselor, Helper, Intercessor, Advocate, Strengthener, Standby), the Holy Spirit, Whom the Father will send in My name [in My place, to represent Me and act on My behalf], **He will teach you all things.** And He will cause you to recall (will remind you of, bring to your remembrance) everything I have told you.*

Romans 8:26 [AMP]
*So too the [Holy] Spirit comes to our aid and bears us up in our weakness; **for we do not know what prayer to offer nor how to offer it worthily as we ought, but the Spirit Himself goes to meet our supplication and pleads in our behalf** with unspeakable yearnings and groanings too deep for utterance.*

The underlined in bold above points to the fact that without the help of the Holy Spirit we will not be able to offer prayers to God effectively. The New King James Version of the Bible uses the phrase help. See Scripture below:

> *Romans 8:26 [NKJV]*
> *Likewise the Spirit also helps in our weaknesses. For we do not know what we should pray for as we ought, but the Spirit Himself makes intercession for us with groaning's which cannot be uttered.*

$$\sim$$

"The eagerness and thirst of praying precedes the how of praying. You must first love prayer or praying before you can learn how to pray."

Hannah's prayer is an example of groaning that could not be uttered. While she was praying only her lips moved but her voice could not be heard. She was praying by the help of the Holy Spirit that she groaned and Eli the priest in the temple thought she was drunk with wine. But Hannah was not drunk with wine, rather her spirit and soul were disconnected from the natural world and in full connection with God's Holy Spirit, *1 Sam 1:15.*

> *1 Samuel 1:12-15 [NKJV]*
> *12 And it happened, as she continued praying before the LORD, that Eli watched her mouth.*
> *13 Now Hannah spoke in her heart; only her lips moved, but her voice was not heard. Therefore Eli*

thought she was drunk.
14 So Eli said to her, "How long will you be drunk?
Put your wine away from you!"
15 But Hannah answered and said, "No, my lord, I
am a woman of sorrowful spirit. I have drunk nei-
ther wine nor intoxicating drink, but have poured
out my soul before the LORD.

The thirst for prayer

Now seeing our prayer know how rests on the Holy Spirit, we must be thirsty first for prayer for the Holy Spirit to teach us how to pray. The Holy Spirit will not teach us anything that we are not interested in. Simply put, the Holy Spirit does not teach thirst(less) folks. Remember that Jesus taught His disciples how to pray after they desired it, *Luke 11:1.*

True and pure thirst for prayer is the driving force behind knowing how to pray, because thirst always releases God's anointing and blessings (empowerment to know how, and to produce result). God said He will pour water and His Spirit upon the thirsty soul;

Isaiah 44:3 [AMP]
For I will pour water upon him who is thirsty, and floods upon the dry ground. I will pour My Spirit upon your offspring, and My blessing upon your descendants.

~

"The Holy Spirit will not teach us anything that we are not interested in."

Pray earnestly and fervently

The Word of God tells us to pray earnestly [heartfelt or engaging our spirit] and fervently [very hot, glowing, exhibiting or marked by great intensity of feeling]. Earnest and fervent prayers make tremendous impact and produce tremendous results.

> *James 5:16-17 [NKJV]*
> *16 Confess your trespasses to one another, and pray for one another, that you may be healed. <u>The effective, fervent prayer of a righteous man avails much.</u>*
> *17 Elijah was a man with a nature like ours, and <u>he prayed earnestly</u> that it would not rain; and it did not rain on the land for three years and six months.*

Earnest and fervent prayers are prayers that involve the whole man, that is: spirit soul and body. Let's revisit the Hannah's prayer; it was an earnest prayer because her spirit, soul, and body were engaged in the prayer. The Bible says that she wept sore and was in bitterness of soul and prayed in that condition by pouring out her soul before God.

> *1 Samuel 1:10, 12-15 [NKJV]*
> *10 <u>And she was in bitterness of soul, and prayed unto</u>*

the LORD, and wept sore.
12 And it happened, as she continued praying before the LORD, that Eli watched her mouth.
13 Now Hannah spoke in her heart; only her lips moved, but her voice was not heard. Therefore Eli thought she was drunk.
14 So Eli said to her, "How long will you be drunk? Put your wine away from you!"
15 But Hannah answered and said, "No, my lord, I am a woman of sorrowful spirit. I have drunk neither wine nor intoxicating drink, but have poured out my soul before the LORD.

When we pray earnestly, we are disconnected from the realm of the physical and are connected by the Holy Spirit to the realm of the spirit. We become insensitive to our physical environment and happenings around us. It is clear from the above Scripture that Hannah was disconnected from the realm of the physical and was in direct connection with the spirit realm, but Eli was in the physical realm hence he thought Hannah was drunk. Hannah's prayer was a heartfelt [Earnest] prayer because she was praying from her heart while pouring her soul desire for a child to God.

~

"Earnest and fervent prayers make tremendous impact and produce tremendous results."

Another example of a heartfelt fervent prayer recorded in the Bible is Nehemiah's prayer. Nehemiah prayed from his heart to God concerning the deploring condition of Jerusalem and the Israelites. His spirit soul and body were engaged.

> *Nehemiah 1:4 [NKJV]*
> *So it was, when I heard these words that I sat down and wept, and mourned for many days; I was fasting and praying before the God of heaven.*

Let's take a deeper look at Nehemiah's action in the above Bible verse.

He sat down (Physical Body engaged): Nehemiah physical body was engaged. Ernest fervent prayer requires one to be in an environment with less interruption from the physical realm. Places like the church prayer room, prayer retreat centers, Prayer Mountains where one can be left alone to commune with God are some examples where one can engage in intense prayers.

Wept and mourned for days (Soul locked in): Nehemiah soul and body engaged. Nehemiah did not stop at the level of engaging his physical body only, but rather he took it to the next level by engaging his soul [his emotions]. If Nehemiah had stop at the physical level [sat down only] it would have been a mere physical reaction. There are some that will interpret weeping before or while praying to always mean a lack of faith. This is not true because the presence or absence of faith has nothing to do with weeping. Jesus was moved emotionally to the extent that He wept before He prayed for Lazarus to come back to life, *John 11:35, 43*. His emotion had nothing to do with His faith, He prayed, and Lazarus came back to life.

Fasted and prayed (Poured out his heart): Nehemiah spirit was engaged through fasting (fasting sharpens the spirit man), and he involved Heaven by praying. If Nehemiah had stopped at the intense soul level where he mourned for certain days, it would have been a mere emotional encounter. But rather he took it to the highest level of the spirit.

~

"Ernest fervent prayer requires one to be in an environment with less interruption from the physical realm."

Apply God's Word when praying

Our prayers are more effective when we pray in line with God's Word. The Bible tells us in *1 John 5:14* that God hears our prayers when we ask according to His will. God's will is in God's Word. Speaking God's Word over a situation or speaking God's Word back to Him when praying engages God and yields tremendous results. Nehemiah prayed this way by remembering God His Word and he got tremendous results, *Nehemiah 1:4-11*. The entire *Book of Nehemiah* shows the tremendous result, which is the rebuilding of the wall and gate of Jerusalem that resulted from Nehemiah's prayer. Read the entire *Book of Nehemiah* to get the full story. Below are some examples of how to apply God's Word in strategic prayers.

■ 1. **The Word:** All things work for good to all who love God.

> *Romans 8:28 [NKJV]*
> *"And we know that all things work together for good to those who love God, to those who are the called according to His purpose."*

Prayer: Father God, your Word has declared that all things work for good to those who love You. Your Word declares in *John 14:23* that the people who keep your Word are those who love You. Father God I love You because I have accepted Jesus as Lord and Savior of my life and I have yielded myself to your Word. I thank You Lord because whatever I have gone through in the past, or going through right now, or will go through in the future will work for my good and the good of my family in Jesus' Name, Amen.

~

"Our prayers are more effective when we pray in line with God's Word."

■ 2. **The Word:** It shall be well with the righteous.

> *Isaiah 3:10 [NKJV]*
> *"Say to the righteous that it shall be well with*

them, For they shall eat the fruit of their doings."

Prayer: Father God your Word says in *Isaiah 3:10* that it shall be well with the righteous and they shall enjoy the rich rewards they have earned. As a believer [born again], I am righteous because your Word says in *Romans 10:10* that with the heart man believes unto righteousness. Therefore, I declare wellness of spirit, soul, and body over my family in Jesus' Name and we will eat the fruit of our doings. We will not work for nothing in Jesus' Name.

■ 3. **The Word:** No weapon directed against believers shall prevail.

> *Isaiah 54:17 [NIV]*
> *"No weapon forged against you will prevail, and you will refute every tongue that accuses you. This is the heritage of the servants of the Lord, and this is their vindication from me, declares the Lord."*

Prayer: Father God your Word declares in *Isaiah 54:17* that no weapon forged against me shall prevail and every tongue that rises against me in judgment, I shall refute. Thank You Father God because I am a believer and the weapons of Satan and his emissaries cannot prevail against me and my family according to your Word in Jesus' Name. I therefore stand on this Word of God and condemn every voice that rises against my family and I in Jesus' Name, Amen.

■ 4. **The Word:** No barrenness among God's children.

Deuteronomy 7:14 [NKJV]
"You shall be blessed above all peoples; there shall not be a male or female barren among you or among your livestock."

Prayer: Father God your Word says in *Deuteronomy 7:14* that there will be none barren among us including our livestock. I therefore break the yoke of barrenness from my life and family members in Jesus' Name, Amen. I declare all round fruitfulness in my life and all connected to me in Jesus' Name, Amen.

■ **5. The Word:** No untimely death among God's children.

Psalms 118:17 [NIV]
"I will not die but live, and will proclaim what the Lord has done."

Prayer: Father your Word declares in *Psalms 118:17* that I shall not die but live to proclaim your works. Therefore I cancel untimely death from my family in Jesus' Name, Amen.

■ **6. The Word:** Satisfied with long life and salvation.

Psalms 91:16 [NIV]
"With long life I will satisfy him and show him my salvation."

Prayer: Father God your Word says in *Psalms 91:16* that

You will satisfy me with long life and show me your salvation. Therefore I declare over myself and family long life and God's saving grace in Jesus' Name.

■ **7. The Word:** Irreversible blessings

Numbers 23:20 [NKJV]
"Behold, I have received a command to bless; He [God] has blessed, and I cannot reverse it."

Prayer: Father God your Word says in Numbers 23:20 that your blessings upon my life cannot be reversed, thus I am blessed beyond a curse. Therefore, I invoke *Numbers 23:20* over my life and family in Jesus' Name, Amen. Praise God for His untouchable blessings upon my life.

■ **8. The Word:** A sign and a wonder to the world

Isaiah 8:18 [NKJV]
"I and the children whom the Lord has given me! We are for signs and wonders in Israel From the Lord of hosts, Who dwells in Mount Zion"

Psalms 71:7 [NKJV]
"I have become as a wonder to many, But You are my strong refuge."

Prayer: Father God your Word says my children and I are for signs and wonders in this world. Therefore, I declare full manifestation of these Scriptures in my life, spouse and children in Jesus' Name. We are the sign the world will follow and your blessings have made us a wonder to many, thank You Father God for being our strong refuge. Praise God, HALLELUJAH!

Pray in faith

No matter how long and intense a prayer may be, if it is prayed in unbelief [lack of faith], it will yield zero result. The Bible tells us in *Hebrews 11:6 [AMP] "But without faith it is impossible to please and be satisfactory to Him. For whoever would come near to God must [necessarily] believe that God exists and that He is the rewarder of those who earnestly and diligently seek Him [out]."* This means that; it is impossible to communicate with God without faith.

The Bible states clearly that anything done outside faith is sin, *Romans 14:23 [AMP] "...For whatever does not originate and proceed from faith is sin [whatever is done without a conviction of its approval by God is sinful]."* This means that a faithless prayer is a sinful prayer and a sinful prayer is a fruitless prayer even when offered by a believer.

◞

"No matter how long and intense a prayer may be, if it is prayed in unbelief [lack of faith], it will yield zero result."

People often get confused when using *James 5:13-15* during prayers. They tend to focus more on the anointing oil thinking that it is the anointing that heals the sick. Most believers put so much attention in anointing oil to the extent that; until they are anointed with oil during a prayer session, they don't believe the effectiveness of the prayer. Anointing someone during prayer is biblical and in line with the Word of God, however it is not the anointing oil that heals and saves the believer, rather it is the prayer of faith. Let's see *James 5:13-15*.

> *James 5:13-15 [NKJV]*
> *13 Is anyone among you suffering? Let him pray. Is anyone cheerful? Let him sing psalms.*
> *14 Is anyone among you sick? Let him call for the elders of the church, and let them pray over him, anointing him with oil in the name of the Lord.*
> *15 **And the prayer of faith will save the sick**, and the Lord will raise him up. And if he has committed sins, he will be forgiven.*

The Bible verses above in *James 5:13-15* makes it clear in *verse 15* [see bold underlined], that the prayer of faith is what brings healing. This means that you don't need to wait for anointing oil before you pray for the sick. I do not say using anointing oil is bad or wrong, what I mean is; with or without anointing oil—healing is sure if faith is present.

I said earlier in this chapter that one of the ways to pray is by applying God's Word. But it should be noted that applying God's Word without faith would yield zero result.

The Bible tells us that when the Word of God is not mixed with faith whether when praying or otherwise, it will not yield profit. See *Hebrews 4:2* below.

Hebrew 4:2 [KJV]
For unto us was the gospel preached, as well as unto them: but the word preached did not profit them, not being mixed with faith in them that heard it.

Praying in faith means that you first believe that God can do more than what you are about praying for *[Ephesians 3:20]* and see and receive the answer to your request with your eyes of faith before commencing and during the prayer. Jesus says when we pray this way, we will have what we are praying for, *Mark 11:24*. See Scripture quotations below.

Mark 11:24 [NKJV]
Therefore I say to you, whatever things you ask when you pray, believe that you receive them, and you will have them.

Ephesians 3:20 [NKJV]
Now to Him who is able to do exceedingly abundantly above all that we ask or think, according to the power that works in us.

Ephesians 3:20 is a powerful Scripture that helps builds our faith because it gives us the confidence that God will do more than what we ask or think. This means that even when we are unable to speak out our needs, if we meditate on them, God will answer and do above our thoughts.

Pray in the Holy Spirit

Praying in the Holy Spirit is the ability given to believers that allows them to pray in a *supernatural* language. It is also sometimes referred to as praying in tongues, praying in unknown tongues, or praying with your spirit language. Praying in unknown tongues is a gift of the Holy Spirit available to all believing Christians. If you are yet to receive this gift, you can ask for it just like the disciples in *Acts 2:1*.

Praying in the Holy Spirit is how our redeemed human spirit communicates directly with God's Holy Spirit. Intended to be used for more than just communicating with God in prayer, it is also designed to be a power producer to enhance the operation of all the other gifts of the Holy Spirit. *Jude 1:20* tells us that when we pray in the Holy Spirit, our faith is built up.

> *Jude 1:20 [NKJV]*
> *But you, beloved, building yourselves up on your most holy faith, praying in the Holy Spirit.*

Strategic Prayer Points and Declarations

STRATEGIC PRAYER

■ 1. Pray for the gifts of the Holy Spirit to be manifested in and through you, your loved ones and in the body of Christ worldwide for the expansion of the Gospel, *1 Cor-*

inthians 12:7.

■ 2. Pray for God to grant you and your loved one's wisdom so that you will know how to pilot your affairs and know how to direct your prayers in times of need. *James 1:5 [NKJV] If any of you lacks wisdom, let him ask of God, who gives to all liberally and without reproach, and it will be given to him.*

■ 3. Pray that the Word of the Lord may run swiftly and be glorified in your life, your loved ones, your city, nation and the world. *2 Thessalonians 3:1 [NKJV] Finally, brethren, pray for us, that the word of the Lord may run swiftly and be glorified, just as it is with you.*

STRATEGIC DECLARATIONS

■ 1. Father God I receive grace to be steadfast in the faith. I will not be misled by the error of the wicked. *2 Peter 3:17 [NKJV] You therefore, beloved, since you know this beforehand, beware lest you also fall from your own steadfastness, being led away with the error of the wicked.*

■ 2. In the Name of Jesus, I terminate the evil activities of wicked and unreasonable men and women who opposes the Gospel of our Lord and Savior Jesus Christ. *2 Thessalonians 3:2 [NKJV] and that we may be delivered from unreasonable and wicked men; for not all have faith.*

■ 3. In the Name of Jesus, I pull down spiritual wicked

demonic spirits operating in high places over families, towns, cities and nations. I declare their works null and void. *2 Corinthians 10:4-5 [NKJV] For the weapons of our warfare are not carnal but mighty in God for pulling down strongholds, 5 casting down arguments and every high thing that exalts itself against the knowledge of God, bringing every thought into captivity to the obedience of Christ.*

~

Chapter 9
Know How to Pray – Part Two

Pray in the Name of Jesus

Prayers should be made to God the Father, in the Name of Jesus. Jesus said in *John 14:13-14* that if we ask anything in His Name—He will do it. Praying in the Name of Jesus yields tremendous results because, at the Name of Jesus everything else bows or submits. See Scripture reference below.

> *Philippians 2:9-11 [NKJV]*
> *9 Therefore God also has highly exalted Him and given Him the name which is above every name,*
> *10 that at the name of Jesus every knee should bow, of those in heaven, and of those on earth, and of those under the earth,*
> *11 and that every tongue should confess that Jesus Christ is Lord, to the glory of God the Father.*

The importance of praying in the Name of Jesus cannot be overemphasized because Jesus is the one and only way by which anyone can come to God the Father. [See *John 14:6* Scripture below]. There are people who round up their prayers by saying "in the Name of God we pray." Such kind of prayers are fruitless and a waste of time because you cannot pray to God in the Name of God, it must be in the Name of Jesus for it to be answered by God the Father, see Bible Scripture *John 14:13-14* below. This means all prayers must be said in the Name of Jesus.

John 14:6 [NKJV]
Jesus said to him, "I am the way, the truth, and the life. No one comes to the Father except through Me.

John 14:13-14 [NKJV]
13 And whatever you ask in My name, that I will do, that the Father may be glorified in the Son. 14 If you ask anything in My name, I will do it.

There are others who pray in the name of Mary mother of God or "Mary mother of God pray for us" or sometimes uses rosery to pray or perform the sign of the cross or pray using the name of a living or dead religious person. If you are praying this way or you know someone who does, please stop and ask them to stop because is not in the Bible and thus un-strategic.

~

"Praying in the Name of Jesus yields tremendous results because, at the Name of Jesus everything else bows or submits."

Pray in Agreement

If you are praying alone, what comes out of your mouth should agree with what is in your heart. Sometimes, when we are praying, our mouth is saying one thing, but our heart is wondering and pondering on other things like pending bills or business runs for the day etc. Our prayers will be in vain, when our words differ from what is in our hearts. It is like what Jesus said in *Mark 7:6* concerning ineffective worship when the heart and words runs contrary to one another. *Ephesians 3:20*, tells us that God responds not only to what we ask with our mouth, but also what we think;

> *Ephesians 3:20 [NKJV]*
> *Now to Him who is able to do exceedingly abundantly above all that we ask or think, according to the power that works in us.*

When we are praying with others, we should pray in agreement. We should make sure we understand the prayer points we are asked to pray about and pray together following the lead of the prayer leader. I have seen believers joining prayer sessions and saying things that are not in line with the prayer points being prayed for by the team. This is not praying in agreement, it is simply praying in disagreement.

In *Acts 4:24*, the apostles came together and prayed in agreement [one accord] when the chief priest and elders threatened them to stop preaching and performing miracles in the Name of Jesus. Because they prayed in agreement [united in spirit], the place they were gathered was shaken; *Acts 4:31.*

Pray without ceasing

In *Luke 18:1-8*, Jesus told his disciples a parable about a widow who persisted in prayer even when her request was being denied. Jesus did this to show His disciples that they should always pray and not give up. This parable teaches us that when we pray about anything, we should hold on and continue until and even after our request is granted. Many Christians easily get frustrated when the answers to their prayers get delayed. Jesus said that He would expedite the answers to believers who pray persistently without giving up like the widow in the parable. See Bible reference below.

Luke 18:1-8 [NIV]
1 Then Jesus told his disciples a parable to show them that they should always pray and not give up.
2 He said: "In a certain town there was a judge who neither feared God nor cared what people thought.
3 And there was a widow in that town who kept coming to him with the plea, 'Grant me justice against my adversary.'
4 For some time he refused. But finally he said to himself, 'Even though I don't fear God or care what people think,
5 yet because this widow keeps bothering me, I will

see that she gets justice, so that she won't eventually come and attack me!"
6 And the Lord said, "Listen to what the unjust judge says.
7 And will not God bring about justice for his chosen ones, who cry out to him day and night? Will he keep putting them off?
8 I tell you, he will see that they get justice, and quickly. However, when the Son of Man comes, will he find faith on the earth?"

Until God says no to our prayers, we should not stop praying, but since God will not say no to believers who are His children [chosen ones] praying in line with His Word, see verse six to eight above, believers are encouraged to continue praying until and after they get their results.

Praying without ceasing is strategic and effective. In *Acts 12:5-7*, when the apostles prayed without ceasing for Peter who was imprisoned by King Herod, God sent an angel to Peter in the prison and he got his freedom from the death trap of king Herod. See Bible reference below;

Acts 12:5-7 [KJV]
5 Peter therefore was kept in prison: but prayer was made without ceasing of the church unto God for him.
6 And when Herod would have brought him forth, the same night Peter was sleeping between two soldiers, bound with two chains: and the keepers before the door kept the prison.

7 And, behold, the angel of the Lord came upon him, and a light shined in the prison: and he smote Peter on the side, and raised him up, saying, Arise up quickly. And his chains fell off from his hands.

Peter's deliverance was a quick one *(Acts 12:7)* and in line with Jesus promise in *Luke 18:8,* that He would send quick deliverance to those who will pray to Him day and night without ceasing. "Persistent ceaseless prayers, yields quick results."

~

"The importance of praying in the Name of Jesus cannot be overemphasized because Jesus is the One and only way by which anyone can come to God the Father."

Pray in the right atmosphere

Being in the right atmosphere during prayer helps one to avoid distractions. Prayer as we said is talking to God. We cannot be praying and watching television at the same time, or praying to God and talking on the phone to friends at the same time. We have to avoid all forms of distractions. To avoid unnecessary distractions, one has to be in the right environment. The Bible tells us that Jesus always withdrew Himself from His disciples to a quiet place to pray.

Mark 1:35 [NKJV]
Now in the morning, having risen a long while before daylight, He went out and departed to a solitary place; and there He prayed.

Hannah's example we looked at earlier was similar to this. She was in the temple of the Lord at Shiloh on a yearly spiritual retreat, *1 Samuel 1:3-15*. She was separated from all physical distraction. Take note that Hannah's husband, Elkanah and Hannah's mate, Peninnah were not with Hannah when she was praying in the temple. Peninnah is Elkanah other wife who provoked Hannah by her actions because Hannah was barren and in need of a child. If Elkanah and Peninnah were around Hannah, they would have disturbed Hannah and hindered her prayer.

Even Eli the priest was not so close to Hannah because he was seated on the temple post while Hannah was inside the temple. So Hannah created the environment where she can be alone with God with no external distraction. Things like television, cell phones and the like should be turned off or put away while praying because they cause huge distractions.

Pray with a heart of praise

Praising God while praying activates and releases the supernatural to intervene on the natural realm. While in prison, Paul and Silas invoked the supernatural on the natural when they prayed and sang praises to God. This resulted on a great earthquake that shook the foundation of the prison, open the door of the prison, and the chains on their hands were loosed. See Scripture reference below.

> *Acts 16:25-26 [NKJV]*
> *25 But at midnight Paul and Silas were praying and singing hymns to God, and the prisoners were listening to them.*
> *26 Suddenly there was a great earthquake, so that the foundations of the prison were shaken; and immediately all the doors were opened and everyone's chains were loosed.*

~

"Praising God while praying activates and releases the supernatural to intervene on the natural realm."

Strategic Prayer Points and Declarations

STRATEGIC PRAYER

■ 1. Pray that the foundations of prisons (spiritual or physical) restricting you, your loved ones and believers worldwide be shaken by the power of the Holy Spirit in Jesus' Name.

■ 2. Pray that satanic restrictions to the Gospel of Jesus Christ everywhere be removed especially in government functionaries.

■ 3. Pray for unity in the Church worldwide so that churches and ministries will team up and begin to work together for the common cause of the Gospel of Jesus Christ, *John 17:20-21 [NKJV] 20 I do not pray for these alone, but also for those who will believe in Me through their word; 21 that they all may be one, as You, Father, are in Me, and I in You; that they also may be one in Us, that the world may believe that You sent Me.*

STRATEGIC DECLARATIONS

■ 1. According to *Matthew 5:14-16,*

• I am the Light of the world because the life of Jesus Christ is in me. Therefore, I remove everything that tries to obscure my light in Jesus' Name. *John 1:4-5*

• The glory of God in me cannot be hidden because I am set on a hill for others to see.

• I will allow my light to shine by declaring the good news of the Gospel of Jesus anywhere and everywhere.

■ 2. According to *Matthew 15:13*, I root out every plant (seed, thoughts, etc.) in my life and loved ones that has not been planted by God in Jesus' Name.

■ 3. According to *3 John 1:2*, I pray and declare prosperity, sound mind, and sound health over my life and loved ones in Jesus' Name. *3 John 1:2 [NKJV] Beloved, I pray that you may prosper in all things and be in health, just as your soul prospers.*

∽

Chapter 10
The Lord's Prayer –
An Example of Strategic Prayer

A clear example of strategic prayer recorded in the Bible, is Jesus teaching His disciples how to pray in *Luke chapter 11*. Let's take a closer look at this great strategic prayer.

> *Luke 11:1-4 [NKJV]*
> *1 Now it came to pass, as He was praying in a certain place, when He ceased, that one of His disciples said to Him, "Lord, teach us to pray, as John also taught his disciples."*
> *2 So He said to them, "When you pray, say: Our Father in heaven, Hallowed be Your name. Your kingdom come. Your will be done On earth as it is in heaven.*
> *3 Give us day by day our daily bread.*
> *4 And forgive us our sins, For we also forgive every-one who is indebted to us. And do not lead us into temptation, But deliver us from the evil one.*

Verse one is the request from the disciples; they wanted to know how to pray. The prayer layout Jesus gave was to meet their request; this is strategic in the sense that the prayer is deployed to solve a specific request "lack of prayer know how." Jesus breaks down His prayer to different phases. Let's review each prayer phase.

Prayer Directed to the Right Source

Jesus instructed them to pray to Father God. Strategic prayer must be made to the right source for it to be effective. Take note of Jesus Words *"Our Father."* This means we must be sons in order to call God our Father. In this context, a son or daughter is one who is born of God the Father and is following the lead of the Father by daily allowing God the Father's Word to function through him or her, by the help of the Holy Spirit; Christian believers are born of God the Father. See *John 1:13.*

> *John 1:13 [NIV]*
> *Children born not of natural descent, nor of human decision or a husband's will, but born of God.*

> *John 1:13 [AMP]*
> *Who owe their birth neither to bloods nor to the will of the flesh [that of physical impulse] nor to the will of man [that of a natural father], but to God. [They are born of God!]*

Take note of the revelation in the above Scriptures. Once you are born of God [born again], you are no longer under your natural descent of family lineage. The supernatural descent supersedes the natural descent. You must know this else the devil and his demons will take advantage of you by claiming falsehood over you. It is possible for a believer who lacks this knowledge to be manipulated and control by spiritual demons of darkness. I personally witness this while ministering deliverance to a born again Christian lady, see story below.

Some time ago my prayer team and I were praying the prayer of deliverance over a lady who was held in bondage [controlled and manipulated] by a wicked demonic spirit of darkness. As we were praying to God the Father in the Name of Jesus for the demon to let go of her, there was a fierce resistance from the demon spirit. The more we prayed, the more the resistance increased to the extent that the demon spoke through the lady these words: *"She is mine, I cannot let her go, I am her mother, I gave birth to her, while I was pregnant with her, I dedicated her to the demon controlling me and as such she is mine."*

Immediately I heard these words, I asked my assistant to open to *John 1:13*. I read *John 1:13* and declared to the demon spirit speaking through her that he [demon spirit] was no longer in charge of the lady's life but rather, Jesus is now in charge because the lady is born of God, not of the will of anybody or demons. As soon as I declared these words, the demon spirit spoke again through the lady the following words: *"I know, I will let go of her."*

Immediately, the fierce resistance from the demon and struggle of the lady ceased and the demon came out of her.

There was a great calm and the lady was quiet for about 30 minutes. Afterwards, the lady stood up and came back to her senses. When we asked her about those demonic claims over her coming out of her mouth, she never remembered saying them. She was delivered of the demonic stronghold of darkness because of strategic praying, after years of manipulation and control by demons of darkness.

After the deliverance, I pondered on the words *"I know, I will let go of her"* spoken by the demonic spirit after I declared the Word of God in *John 1:13*. It is clear that the demonic spirit new her to be a born again child of God, but was acting on her ignorance of the Word of God.

Prayer Started with Praise

Hallowed be thy Name is offering praises to God. Jesus taught His disciples to start their prayers with praises and offering of thanks to God. Praises and offering of thanks moves God to act quickly. Before praying for Lazarus to come back to life, Jesus offered thanks first to God, *John 11:41-43*. Praises not only move God to act quickly, it also puts God in charge of the situation at hand. This was the case of Jehoshaphat as recorded in *2 Chronicles 20:21-22;*

2 Chronicle 20:21-22 [NKJV]
21 And when he had consulted with the people, he appointed those who should sing to the Lord, and who should praise the beauty of holiness, as they went out before the army and were saying: "Praise

the Lord, For His mercy endures forever."
22 Now when they began to sing and to praise, the Lord set ambushes against the people of Ammon, Moab, and Mount Seir, who had come against Judah; and they were defeated.

Note that as they began to sing praises, it was God Who set ambush against the people of Amon, Moab, and Mount Seir. That is, God took over the fight and the enemy fought against themselves and destroy themselves. Jehoshaphat and his people never fought in this battle. When our praises go up to God, He [God] comes down into our affairs and takes the lead because according to *Psalms 22:3 [KJV] God inhabits the praise of His people.* We should learn how to give God high praise always, even at the peak of our struggles and challenges.

~

"Praises not only move God to act quickly, it also puts God in charge of the situation at hand."

Prayer Continued with Release of God's System of Government

The next phase of the prayer as taught by Jesus, is *"thy kingdom come,"* Thy will be done on Earth as in Heaven." Thy Kingdom come is inviting God's system of governing to invade the earth and Thy will be done is asking and releasing God's desires over the nations of the earth. This phase of the prayer is strategic in the sense that when God's system and desire is deployed on Earth, it replaces and paralyses Satan's system and desires.

~

"When our praises go up to God, He [God] comes down into our affairs and takes the lead."

Prayer continued with asking

The next phase of prayer Jesus taught was *"give us this day our daily bread."* After praise and inviting God to take the lead in our affairs, Jesus said we could now ask for specific personal or family needs. It is unfortunate that most believers pray un-strategically because the first thing in their line of prayer is always asking God for something. There is nothing wrong in asking during prayers; in fact, Jesus encourages us to ask as seen in *Matthew 7:7 "Ask it shall be given you, seek you will find, knock the door shall be open for you."* Asking and receiving occupies an important part in every prayer. However, our prayers should not only be about asking and receiving.

Prayer continued with mercy and love

Jesus ushered in mercy and love in His strategic prayer teaching by adding, *"Forgive us our sins as we forgive those indebted to us." "Forgive us our sins"* ushers in mercy while *"as we forgive those indebted to us"* ushers in love. It is true that as sons and daughters of God, our sins have been forgiven us because the blood of Jesus has washed us. However, we should ask for forgiveness anytime we consciously or even unconsciously err and deviate from God's unfailing grace. As believers, if we don't ask for forgiveness when we consciously or unconsciously err or deviate from God's unfailing and ever-present grace, we deceive ourselves and the truth of God's Word is not in us.

> *1 John 1:8-10 [NKJV]*
> *8 If we say that we have no sin, we deceive ourselves, and the truth is not in us.*
> *9 If we confess our sins, He is faithful and just to forgive us our sins and to cleanse us from all unrighteousness.*
> *10 If we say that we have not sinned, we make Him a liar, and His word is not in us.*

Prayer continued with God's guidance and deliverance

Jesus went on by teaching them to always ask for guidance from God, *"Lead us not into temptation and deliver us from the evil one."*

Strategic Prayer Points and Declarations

STRATEGIC PRAYER

■ 1. Pray that your life will manifest God's glory and that songs of praise to God will always fill your heart, mind

and mouth in Jesus' Name. *Isaiah 43:21 [NKJV] This people I have formed for Myself; They shall declare My praise.*

■ 2. Pray that the grace to forgive people when they of-
fend you comes on you [Father God I receive grace to forgive whenever I am offended in Jesus' Name]. *Matthew
6:14 [NIV] 14 For if you forgive other people when they sin
against you, your heavenly Father will also forgive you. 15
But if you do not forgive others their sins, your Father will
not forgive your sins.*

■ 3. Pray for God's guidance daily and that you and your
loved ones will not be lead into temptation and you all
will be delivered from the evil one. *Luke 11:4 [NKJV] "…
And do not lead us into temptation, But deliver us from the
evil one"*

STRATEGIC DECLARATIONS

■ 1. Father God I am created to show forth your praise
and that is what will continue to manifest in my life from
now on in Jesus' Name, *Isaiah 43:21.*

■ 2. Father God I depend on you for my daily supply and
as such I will never lack in Jesus' Name because you are
my Jehovah El-Shaddai [The all sufficient God]. *2 Corinthians 3:5 Not that we are sufficient of ourselves to think
of anything as being from ourselves, but our sufficiency is
from God.*

■ 3. Father God I am embedded in you because I am your child and will continue to dwell in your secret place. *Psalms 91:1 [NKJV] He who dwells in the secret place of the Most High Shall abide under the shadow of the Almighty.*

∼

Chapter 11
Fasting and Strategic Prayer

Strategic praying will be incomplete if we fail to talk of the part fasting plays in our prayers. Fasting and prayer are like twin brothers, they are both spiritual weapons of war that complement one another. Most of the prayers recorded in the Bible that yielded immediate result were done with fasting. Below are some examples of break-through strategic prayers deployed with fasting as recorded in the Bible.

Jehoshaphat

When Jehoshaphat got the news of the advancement of the enemy, the first thing he did is to proclaim a fast in all Judah (see bold underline in verse three below), and he asks the people of Judah to seek the Lord God (see verse four below). The word "seek the Lord" means to pray to God for help.

2 Chronicles 20:2-4 [NKJV]
2 Then some came and told Jehoshaphat, saying, "A great multitude is coming against you from beyond

the sea, from Syria; and they are in Hazazon Tamar"
(which is En Gedi).
3 And Jehoshaphat feared, and set himself to seek the
Lord, and __proclaimed a fast__ throughout all Judah.
4 So Judah gathered together to ask help from the
Lord; and from all the cities of Judah they came to
seek the Lord.

When you read the entire chapter, you see that God gave Jehoshaphat victory over his enemy. Adding fasting to our prayers when we are faced with challenges brings victory. On many occasion, I have gotten expedited answers when I deployed my prayers in faith with fasting.

~

"Most of the prayers recorded in the Bible that yielded immediate result were done with fasting."

Esther

When the Jews were faced with annihilation, Esther embarked on a three-day absolute fast and found favor in the sight of the king on the third day of her fast when she appeared in the king's palace without an invitation. This means fasting helps in releasing God's favor. See Scriptures below.

Esther 4:16 [NKJV]
Go, gather all the Jews who are present in Shushan,

and fast for me; neither eat nor drink for three days, night or day. My maids and I will fast likewise. And so I will go to the king, which is against the law; and if I perish, I perish.

Esther 5:1-2 [NKJV]
1 Now it happened on the third day that Esther put on her royal robes and stood in the inner court of the king's palace, across from the king's house, while the king sat on his royal throne in the royal house, facing the entrance of the house.
2 So it was, when the king saw Queen Esther standing in the court, that she found favor in his sight, and the king held out to Esther the golden scepter that was in his hand. Then Esther went near and touched the top of the scepter.

What is Fasting?

Fasting is primarily the act of abstaining from all food, drink, fleshly pleasures, etc. for a set period for spiritual empowerment. See *Esther 4:16*, and *Matthew 4:2*.

Types of Fasting

▶ Absolute or Total Fast

An absolute or total fast is normally defined as abstinence from all food, liquid, fleshly pleasures for a defined period, usually a single day, or few days. Absolute fast should not be done longer than what the body could handle. Serious health issues can result when the body is devoid of required nutrients for too long a time than necessary. For more information on body nutrition requirements, consult your nutritionist.

The Bible has record of the following absolute fast; Moses in *Exodus 24:18,* Esther in *Esther 4:16,* Jesus in *Matthew 4:1.* Spiritual and medical counsel should be sought before embarking on a long absolute fast. I recommend taking water during absolute fast because it helps in cleansing of the body. Taking water does not break a fast.

▶ **Daily Fast**

This is the type of fast where one skips one or two meals a day for several days, as much as the body can handle. Taking water during daily fast is a good idea as it helps to clean the body system. As I explained above, water does not break a fast.

⁓

"Adding fasting to our prayers when we are faced with challenges brings victory."

Why Fasting?

1. Fasting helps you to humble your soul. *Psalms 35:13 (NKJV) "But as for me, when they were sick, My clothing was sackcloth; I humbled myself with fasting; And my prayer would return to my own heart."*

2. Makes your spirit to be alert and sensitive to God's Holy Spirit. *Acts 13:2 (NKJV) "As they ministered to the Lord and fasted, the Holy Spirit said, Now separate to Me Barnabas and Saul for the work to which I have called them."*

3. Destroys the networks of spiritual wicked forces of darkness. *Isaiah 58:6 (NKJV) "Is this not the fast that I have chosen: To loose the bonds of wickedness, To undo the heavy burdens, To let the oppressed go free, And that you break every yoke."* Note that it is not the fasting that does the destruction but rather the power of the Holy Spirit already in you. But this power of the Holy Spirit can be deployed more effectively when our spirit is alert and sharp, and fasting helps achieve that.

4. Overturn the enemy's plan. Haman's plot to kill the Jews was overturned after Esther went on a three-day fasting. The gallows Haman dogged for Mordecai was where he ended up hanged. *Esther 4:16 (NKJV) "Go, gather all the Jews who are present in Shushan, and fast for me; neither eat nor drink for three days, night or day. My maids and I will fast likewise. And so I will go to the king, which is against the law; and if I perish, I perish." Esther 7:10 (NKJV) "So they hanged Haman on the gallows that he had prepared for Mordecai. Then the king's wrath subsided."*

5. Brings healing to the physical body. Fasting, when done properly, releases healing in our physical body, see *Isaiah*

58:8, read *verses 6-8* for more clarity. *Isaiah 58:8 [NKJV] Then your light shall break forth like the morning, Your healing shall spring forth speedily, And your righteousness shall go before you; The glory of the Lord shall be your rear guard.*

Who Fasting is for?

Fasting is for all humans if your health condition can allow you. Children who have attained the age of understanding should be trained how to fast. At least one meal fasting as the child can bear. *Joel 2:15-17*

Why Fasting is neglected these days

● The Ignorance Factor

The majority of Christians lack the knowledge of what fasting, and prayer can do in their lives. In *Mark 9:28*, the disciples came to Jesus privately and ask why they could not cast out a dumb spirit. Prior to this in *Mark 9:19*, Jesus had chastised them for their lack of faith, but it is important to note that their lack of faith is not the only thing Jesus spoke about, rather He explained further to them in *verse 29*, that; *"this kind comes forth by nothing but by prayer and fasting."* This means that the disciples were ignorant of the power of fasting and prayer.

● The Flesh Factor

The reason why some Christians find it difficult to fast and pray even when they know what fasting and prayer can do, is because they are still being ruled by the desires of the flesh like food, sex, sleep, and other worldly pleasures that feeds the flesh. Fasting and prayer, coupled with studying the Word of God, feeds and energizes the human spirit. Although fasting and prayer with the Word of God energizes the spirit, it is carried out by the physical body "flesh", and because the desire of the flesh is opposed to the desires of the spirit, the flesh will always want to resist the call to fasting and prayer. *Galatians 5:17 (NKJV) "For the flesh lusts against the Spirit, and the Spirit against the flesh; and these are contrary to one another, so that you do not do the things that you wish."*

The human flesh is controlled by the physical senses of seeing, smelling, feeling, hearing, and touching. We can control the desires of our flesh by living and walking in the spirit. *Galatians 5:16 (NKJV) "I say then: Walk in the Spirit, and you shall not fulfill the lust of the flesh."* The word *"lust"* means "intense desire or craving," that is; what controls the flesh or the cravings of the flesh. These are the physical senses described above. All true Christians have crucified the flesh with the affections and desires, *Galatians 5:24*. Yielding ourselves to the leading of the Holy Spirit on a daily basis will help us put our flesh under control and help our spirit take the lead.

● The Wrong Concept Factor

Most Christians believe fasting and prayer are only meant for Pastors, Ministers, and the like. Some even believe

fasting and prayer to be a special ministry meant for se-
lected few. This is not true because fasting and prayer is
meant for all born again children of God. The Bible men-
tions the following people from all walks of life that were
involved in fasting and praying:

- **Queens:** Queen Esther and all the Jews, *Esther 4:16*

- **Servants:** Queen Esther maidens, *Esther 4:16*

- **Kings:** King David, *Psalms 109:24, 35:13*

- **Captives:** Prince Daniel, *Daniel 10:2, 3*

- **Government officials:** Nehemiah, *Nehemiah 1:4*

- **Elders and children:** *Joel 2:15, 16*

- **Prophets:** Prophetess Anna, *Luke 2:37*

- **Apostles:** The Apostles, *Acts 13:3*

- **Our Lord and Savior:** Jesus Christ, *Matthew 4:2*

Wow! There is no limit to the above list. Fasting and praying is for every child of God—including you. There are
those that contract out their fasting and prayers by asking
others to fast and pray on their behalf and giving money
or other gifts in return. This act is not biblical and should
be discouraged. The only time one should solicit others to
fast and pray for him without himself taking part is when
his physical body is afflicted to the extent where he is unable to carry out any form of fasting and effective prayers.
A few Christians believe that their tithes and offerings can

be a substitute for fasting and prayers. If you fall in this category, please repent. No doubt, payment of tithes and giving offerings attracts God blessings; however, they cannot be used as a substitute for fasting and prayers.

Others have the wrong concept of age limit, especially when it comes to fasting. There is no age limit to fasting, if your physical body can carry you, keep on until the Lord calls you home. The Bible made mention of one Anna, a prophetess and widow of 84 years, who served the Lord with fasting and prayers day and night in the temple. This proves there is no age limit.

Luke 2:36-37 [NKJV]
36 Now there was one, Anna, a prophetess, the daughter of Phanuel, of the tribe of Asher. She was of a great age, and had lived with a husband seven years from her virginity;
37 And this woman was a widow of about eighty-four years, who did not depart from the temple, but served God with fasting's and prayers night and day.

～

"Yielding ourselves to the leading of the Holy Spirit on a daily basis will help us put our flesh under control and help our spirit take the lead."

● **The No Time Factor**

Some people complain of not having the time to dedicate to fasting and praying, citing business and work schedule as a factor. You don't need to take a vacation to commence a fast or to pray. You can be involved in fasting while going about your daily business. Paul said in the *Book of Philippians 4:13 "I can do all things through Christ which strengthens me."* All things referred to in this Scripture include fasting and prayer.

Strategic Prayer Points and Declarations

STRATEGIC PRAYER

■ 1. Pray that the grace to enable you live a fasting life be release on you in Jesus' Name.

■ 2. Pray the below points over your life, loved ones, city, nation. *Isaiah 58:6 [NKJV] "Is this not the fast that I have chosen: To loose the bonds of wickedness, To undo the heavy burdens, To let the oppressed go free, And that you break every yoke."*

- Loose the bands of wickedness in Jesus' Name.

- Undo heavy burdens in Jesus' Name.

- Let the oppressed go free in Jesus' Name.

- Break every yoke in Jesus' Name.

■ 3. Pray that fleshy desires of lust and sexual immorality be put to death in your body in Jesus' Name. *Colossians 3:5 [NIV] Put to death, therefore, whatever belongs to your earthly nature: sexual immorality, impurity, lust, evil desires and greed, which is idolatry.*

STRATEGIC DECLARATIONS

■ 1. I will not die before my time. I will live and declare the works of Jesus Christ to the world. *Psalms 118:17 [NKJV] I shall not die, but live, and declare the works of the Lord.*

■ 2. Because the Lord is my refuge and dwelling place, no harm or disaster will overtake me and my loved ones in Jesus' Name. *Psalms 91:9-10 [NIV] If you say, "The Lord is my refuge," and you make the Most High your dwelling, 10 no harm will overtake you, no disaster will come near your tent.*

■ 3. My star will not diminish in brightness because You have made my path as the shining sun, shining ever brighter unto a perfect day. *Proverbs 4:18 [NKJV] But the path of the just is like the shining sun, that shines ever brighter unto the perfect day.*

～

Chapter 12
Kinds of Prayers

In *Ephesians 6:18*, the Bible tells us to pray on all occasions with all kinds of prayers and requests (see bold in Bible verse below). This means that for our prayers to be effective, we must understand the different kinds of prayer talked about in the Bible. This will enable us to know the right prayer to deploy in times of need.

> *Ephesians 6:18 [NIV]*
> *And pray in the Spirit on all occasions with **all kinds of prayers and requests**. With this in mind, be alert and always keep on praying for all the Lord's people.*

Before going into kinds of prayer, it is imperative to re-emphasize that for our prayers to be strategic and effective, that is; yielding the expected results, they must be offered under certain conditions no matter the kind of prayer being offered. Below are three conditions by which all prayers, if offered—will yield the God desired result.

■ **1. In Love,** without offenses – that is, with a heart of forgiveness. Jesus said in *Mark 11:25-26 (NKJV)* "*25 And whenever you stand praying, if you have anything against anyone, forgive him, that your Father in heaven may also forgive you your trespasses. 26 But if you do not forgive, neither will your Father in heaven forgive your trespasses.*"

■ **2. In faith** – believe you have received your request before commencement of prayer and begin to act on it immediately after the prayer. Jesus said in *Mark 11:24 (NKJV)* "*Therefore I say to you, whatever things you ask when you pray, believe that you receive them, and you will have them.*" The words "*whatever things you ask when you pray*" is the type of prayer, while "*believe you receive them*" is the prayer offered in faith.

■ **3. In agreement** with the Word of God. *James 4:3 (NKJV)* "*You ask and do not receive, because you ask amiss (wrongly), that you may spend it on your pleasures.*" All prayer kinds must be offered in line with the Word of God. Praying for your enemies to die is not in agreement with the Word of God, because Jesus said we should love our enemies and pray for those who spitefully use and persecute us, *Matthew 5:44 (NKJV)* "*But I say to you, love your enemies, bless those who curse you, do good to those who hate you, and pray for those who spitefully use you and persecute you.*"

Prayer of Salvation

This is the most important prayer a person will ever say. This is the prayer offered by the unbeliever. It is the prayer that transforms the sinner (unbeliever) from death to life eternal. *Romans 10:9-10* tell us how the prayer of salvation should be offered or administered.

~

"...for our prayers to be effective, we must understand the different kinds of prayer talked about in the Bible."

Romans 10:9-10 [NKJV]
9 That if you confess with your mouth the Lord Jesus and believe in your heart that God has raised Him from the dead, you will be saved.
10 For with the heart one believes unto righteousness, and with the mouth confession is made unto salvation.

Salvation Prayer

"Dear Jesus, I believe in my heart that You died and was buried, and God raised You from the dead for my salvation. I repent from my sins and receive forgiveness, and I confess with my mouth your Lordship over my life. Thank you, Father God, for sending your Son Jesus for my salvation, in Jesus' Name I pray, Amen."

Prayer of Repentance

The prayer of repentance is the prayer offered by a believer who by commission or omission sins against God. The prayer of repentance requires confessing one's sins or the sins of others for forgiveness. The Word of God tells us in *1 John 1:9 (NIV) "If we confess our sins, he is faithful and just and will forgive us our sins and purify us from all unrighteousness."* Also, *James 5:16* tells us to confess our sins to one another and pray for one another for healing. Nehemiah prayed the prayer of repentance while interceding for the sins of his fathers. Nehemiah's prayer was a combination of the prayer of intercession and repentance because he was praying both for himself and the nation of Israel. See Scripture below.

Nehemiah 1:6 [NKJV]
Please let Your ear be attentive and Your eyes open, that You may hear the prayer of Your servant which I pray before You now, day and night, for the children of Israel Your servants, and confess the sins of the children of Israel which we have sinned against You. Both my father's house and I have sinned.

Prayer of Praise & Thanksgiving

This is the prayer dedicated primarily for offering praise and thanks to God without asking anything from Him. *Hebrews 13:15 (NKJV) "Therefore by Him let us continually offer the sacrifice of praise to God, that is, the fruit of our lips, giving thanks to His name."* The prayer of praise and thanksgiving is praising and thanking God for what He has done, what He is doing, and what He will do in the future. Jesus prayed the prayer of thanksgiving at the tomb site of Lazarus when He said, *"Father I thank You for always hearing me in prayer." (John 11:41-42)*.

~

"Believe you have received your request before commencement of prayer and begin to act on it immediately after the prayer."

Prayer of Consecration

This is praying God's will over a situation and rescinding your will (Note: God's will is revealed in His Word). Prayer of consecration does not mean the absence of faith as some may imply it to be; rather it is simply placing your faith in God knowing fully well that God's will concerning you is good and not evil, to give you your expected end in line with His Word. The Bible tells us that God's thoughts toward us are good and not evil to give us a future hope. See *Jeremiah 29:11* below.

> *Jeremiah 29:11 [NKJV]*
> *For I know the thoughts that I think toward you, says the Lord, thoughts of peace and not of evil, to give you a future and a hope.*

Wonderful! Isn't it? I mean the above Scripture; yes, it is wonderful because it makes us know absolutely that rescinding our will to God's will is the best. Jesus did the same when He prayed the prayer of consecration in Gethsemane and the result was divine intervention from Heaven, an angel strengthening Him, and He was able to pray more intensely. See Bible Scripture below;

> Luke 22:41-44 [NKJV]
> 41 And He was withdrawn from them about a stone's throw, and He knelt down and prayed,
> 42 saying, "Father, if it is your will, take this cup away from Me; nevertheless not My will, but Yours, be done."
> 43 Then an angel appeared to Him from heaven, strengthening Him.
> 44 And being in agony, He prayed more earnestly.

If you have been praying for the salvation or deliverance of a loved one and you are yet to see the answer come to manifestation, that is; it looks like there is a delay, surrender him or her to God for His will to be done. At the expected time, in God's timetable for that loved one there will be a change in Jesus' Name, Amen.

The Prayer of Deliverance

This is the kind of prayer offered when one is under captivity of any sort. The captivity may be spiritual or physical. Spiritual captivity is also called demonic possession. This is the situation where a person becomes possessed and controlled by a demonic spirit. The primary purpose of the prayer of deliverance is to set one free from bondage either spiritually or physically. An example of deliverance prayer in the Bible offered for one in spiritual captivity is the case of deliverance of the child suffering from seizure caused by a demon spirit. This prayer of deliverance was administered by Jesus. See *Matthew 17:14-15, 18* below.

Matthew 17:14 -15, 18 [NIV]
14 When they came to the crowd, a man approached Jesus and knelt before him.
15 "Lord, have mercy on my son," he said. "He has seizures and is suffering greatly. He often falls into the fire or into the water.
18 Jesus rebuked the demon, and it came out of the boy, and he was healed at that moment.

An example of a deliverance prayer recorded in the Bible (for liberation from physical captivity), was the kind of prayer offered by Paul and Silas when they were held captive in prison. Paul and Silas prayed and sang for their personal deliverance, and because of their prayer and praises, there was an earthquake and the prison doors were opened and their chains fell off. See Scripture below.

Acts 16:23-26 [NKJV]
23 And when they had laid many stripes on them, they threw them into prison, commanding the jailer to keep them securely.
24 Having received such a charge, he put them into the inner prison and fastened their feet in the stocks.
25 But at midnight Paul and Silas were praying and

singing hymns to God, and the prisoners were listening to them.
26 Suddenly there was a great earthquake, so that the foundations of the prison were shaken; and immediately all the doors were opened and everyone's chains were loosed.

I have personally been involved in the prayer of deliverance and have seen instant results being manifested in the life of the person(s) prayed for. Some time ago a brother came to me for deliverance from extreme addiction to nicotine. I prayed the prayer of deliverance over him and he was set free from nicotine and never went back to smoking. This may sound too true for some to believe because they think the only way out of strong addiction to nicotine, is going through counseling and programs. Some addictions are spiritually controlled by demonic spirits of darkness and as such—need the prayer of deliverance to break.

Prayer of Authority (Binding and Loosing)

This is a prayer designed to get the devil and his agents out of any situation. *Luke 9:1 (NKJV) "Then He called His twelve disciples together and gave them power and authority over all demons, and to cure diseases." Matthew 18:18 (NKJV) "Assuredly, I say to you, whatever you bind on earth will be bound in heaven, and whatever you loose on earth will be loosed in heaven."* Believers should never negotiate any case with the devil; instead, they should take authority over the devil. There was never a place recorded in the Bible where Jesus or anyone else negotiated with the devil. Some might liken the story in *Matthew 8:31-32* where demons requested to be cast into herd of swine as a form of negotiation. This is not negotiation in anyway because when you read the verses, you notice that the demons begged Jesus saying, *"If you cast us out, permit us to go into the swine."* Now when Jesus responded—He just said *"Go!"*

Prayer of Agreement (United Prayer)

This is a united prayer done by two or more believers. *Matthew 18:19 (NKJV) "Again I say to you that if two of you agree on earth concerning anything that they ask, it will be done for them by My Father in heaven."* The prayer of agreement and intercession was put into practice by the apostles when Peter was arrested and jailed by Herod, *Acts 12:5 (NIV) "So Peter was kept in prison, but the church was earnestly praying to God for him."* Peter's arrest and imprisonment united the Church in agreement to pray for him and as a result, God sent an angel to the prison and Peter was rescued from the prison *(Acts 12:6-11)*.

Sometime ago one of my ministers fell seriously sick to the point of death because of high blood pressure. His kidney packed up and he bled profusely from his nose. His condition was so bad that the doctors gave up on him. At one point for a short time (as he testified afterwards), he literally passed on and saw his spirit wandering among the dead. But during all this time, the church was united praying intensely without ceasing for him to be restored back. United prayers were offered for him at the hospital, the church, in our homes, and over prayer lines on both daily and weekly basis. God heard our prayers and he was healed and restored back to life! Praise God.

~

"Believers should never negotiate any case with the devil; instead, they should take authority over the devil."

Prayer of Intercession

The prayer of intercession is praying for another person, group of people, or nation for their salvation, healing, deliverance, blessings, etc. It is another very important prayer kind because it is selfless. It is praying the other kinds of prayer—for others. Paul emphasized the importance of intercession prayer (as written in the *Book of 1 Timothy 2:1-2)* when he said it should be among the first prayer kind to be offered. See Scripture verse below.

> *1 Timothy 2:1-2 [NIV]*
> *1 I urge, then, first of all, that petitions, prayers, intercession and thanksgiving be made for all people."*
> *2 For kings and all those in authority, that we may live peaceful and quiet lives in all godliness and holiness.*

Instead of criticizing leadership and authority placed

over us as it is commonly and constantly being done, we should rather in love intercede for them for peace, godliness, and holiness. Love is the driving force behind intercession prayers because it helps you pray for your enemies and those who hate and speak evil of you *(Matthew 5:44)*. Moses interceded for his sister Miriam for her healing and restoration from leprosy. *Numbers 12:13 [NKJV] "So Moses cried out to the Lord, saying, "Please heal her, O God, I pray."* The leprosy came on Miriam after she and Aaron spoke against Moses. See *Numbers 12:1-10*. Rather than holding it against Miriam, Moses interceded for her restoration and God heard and restored Miriam.

The prayer of intercession is the primary prayer constantly being offered by Jesus on behalf of believers. *Romans 8:34 [NKJV] "Who is he who condemns? It is Christ who died, and furthermore is also risen, who is even at the right hand of God, who also makes intercession for us."* Hebrews *7:25 [NKJV] "Therefore He is also able to save to the uttermost those who come to God through Him, since He always lives to make intercession for them."* If Jesus is constantly praying for us (believers), we should never give up praying for our loved ones no matter how bad the case might be, because there is no case too bad for God to turn around for His glory. We are to pray for God to spare the souls of our loved ones from destruction (as written in the *Book of Joel 2:17)*. See Scripture below.

Joel 2:17 [NKJV]
Let the priests, who minister to the Lord, Weep between

the porch and the altar; Let them say, "Spare your people, O Lord, and do not give your heritage to reproach, that the nations should rule over them. Why should they say among the peoples, 'Where is their God?"

～

"Love is the driving force behind intercession prayers because it helps you pray for your enemies and those who hate and speak evil of you."

Prayer of Remembrance

The prayer of remembrance is the kind of prayer by which a believer in humility prays by pointing to God's Word or personal sacrifice he or she has rendered in the Kingdom of God as a means of finding favor with God. This means if a person does not have any personal sacrificial contribution towards God's Kingdom, he or she will have nothing to point to for God to remember. Some may think praying this way amounts to pride or an indication that God has forgotten. No, it is not an indication of pride or because God may have forgotten, but rather a fulfillment of Scriptures. God said in His Word that we should put Him in remembrance when pleading our case (when praying), *Isaiah 43:26 "Put Me in remembrance; Let us contend together; State your case, that you may be acquitted."* The prayer of remembrance is the prayer Hezekiah prayed when he was faced with death in *2 Kings 20:2-3 "2 Then he turned his face toward the wall, and prayed to the Lord, saying, 3 Remember now, O Lord, I pray, how I have walked before You in truth and with a loyal heart, and have done what was good in Your sight. And Hezekiah wept bitterly."* Hezekiah's prayer was answered as seen in *2 Kings 20:4-6.*

Strategic Prayer Points and Declarations

STRATEGIC PRAYER

■ 1. Pray that God will remember you, your loved ones, city and nation at the appointed time according to His Word for His purpose to be fulfilled. *Genesis 8:1 Then God remembered Noah, and every living thing, and all the animals that were with him in the ark. And God made a wind to pass over the earth, and the waters subsided.*

■ 2. Pray that your faith and the faith of your loved ones will not fail in the times of trials and temptation. *Luke 22:31-32 [NKJV] 31 And the Lord said, "Simon, Simon! Indeed, Satan has asked for you, that he may sift you as wheat. 32 But I have prayed for you, that your faith should not fail; and when you have returned to Me, strengthen your brethren.*

■ 3. Pray the points listed below over your life, loved ones, city and nation. *Ezekiel 12:22-23 22 [NKJV] "Son of man, what is this proverb that you people have about the land of Israel, which says, 'The days are prolonged, and every vi-*

sion fails'? 23 Tell them therefore, 'Thus says the Lord God: "I will lay this proverb to rest, and they shall no more use it as a proverb in Israel."' But say to them, "'The days are at hand, and the fulfillment of every vision.

- Every negative and evil proverb cease immediately in Jesus' Name.

- Restoration of every failed vision in Jesus' Name.

- Fulfilment of every God given vision in Jesus' Name.

- Prolonged seasons be normalized immediately in Jesus' Name.

STRATEGIC DECLARATIONS

■ 1. The Lord Jesus is the source of all my supply. Therefore I shall not lack anything good. *Philippians 4:19 [NKJV] And my God shall supply all your need according to His riches in glory by Christ Jesus.*

■ 2. Where others have failed, I will prevail. In the eyes of those who are expecting me to fail, I will excel in Jesus' Name. *1 Chronicles 5:1-2*

■ 3. I declare an utter end to all afflictions facing me and my loved ones in Jesus' Name. *Nahum 1:9*

■ 4. I command gates lifted and I usher God's glory into my life and the life of my loved ones in Jesus' Name. *Psalms 24:7*

■ 5. I shut every satanic doors and open doors of victory, progress, success, joy, accomplishment, completion, fulfillment and the like into my life and the life of my loved ones in Jesus' Name. *Revelations 3:7*

Check out all the Great Books from
BOLD TRUTH PUBLISHING

www.ingramcontent.com/pod-product-compliance
Lightning Source LLC
LaVergne TN
LVHW021459080426
835509LV00018B/2340